A Daughter is Special

A Daughter is Special

Mridula Sinha

Translated by

Meenakshi Sinha

PRABHAT
PAPERBACKS

Published by
PRABHAT PAPERBACKS
An imprint of Prabhat Prakashan Pvt. Ltd.
4/19 Asaf Ali Road,
New Delhi-110002 (INDIA)
e-mail: prabhatbooks@gmail.com

ISBN 978-93-5521-006-7
A DAUGHTER IS SPECIAL
by Smt. Mridula Sinha

Edition
First, 2022

Price
₹ 300.00 (Rupees Three Hundred only)

Printed at
R-Tech Offset Printers, Delhi

To those daughters who were special,
are special, and will always remain special

Translator's Note

Dear Mom,

This book started with a letter you wrote to me on my 25th birthday. I am writing this letter to you on my 45th birthday. I did not expect you to not be with me on this day. How can we ever imagine a parent to not be around? You left us unexpectedly on November 18th of last year (2020). This has been a very hard year for me, for everyone in our family. We are still in shock, in disbelief, and sometimes in denial that you are gone. You, with your larger-than-life personality, your deep personal connections with everyone you loved, your ambitious plans for the future—how can you be gone? Your memories are slowly filling up the deep void created in our lives by your departure.

I did not get to see you in your last days. We spoke on the phone on the day of Diwali, on November 14th. How full of energy and excitement your voice had been that day! You blessed me, Ranveer, and Radhika more profusely than ever before. That very night you had a heart attack. After your surgery you were on life support. I was here in America and did not get a chance to speak with you, see you, or touch you. You were gone four days later. I have wondered often since then—what would you have said to me if you were conscious and not on the ventilator? What would your last words have been if you could speak? I will never know.

As I picked up this book of yours a few months later, I

realized that you had already said to me—written to me—everything you wanted to. These letters speak to me your words, your love for me, your belief in me. These letters reassure me that your essence is with me forever, even if your body is not.

Mom, thank you for leaving this invaluable treasure for me. These letters contain so many stories—stories from my childhood, your childhood, stories you picked up from your travels around the world, and stories of remarkable characters from Hindu mythology. All these stories offer valuable insights and lessons drawn from our rich Indian heritage. The scriptures, the social customs and order, festivities and rituals, family values and relationships—everything you were a living and thriving example of, is contained in these letters. You wanted the letters to reach many daughters, not just me. And not just daughters, but mothers, fathers, and sons too. You wanted me to be proud of our Indian heritage and to share our culture and traditions with all my friends in America. You wanted me to teach my daughter Radhika everything you taught me.

That is why I felt the need to translate the letters into English. Now many more people, both in India and abroad, can read the letters. Many of my friends, both Indians and non-Indians, have been waiting eagerly for the English version to share with their daughters. For first generation Indian immigrants in America like me, this book is very relatable. It is relatable also for all mothers who have experienced sending their daughters off to a foreign land, for mothers who have spent sleepless nights worrying about a daughter crossing the socially acceptable marriageable age, and for fathers who share a precious bond with their daughters. I know many people will find the book interesting and educational, and I do hope it reaches a wide audience as you wanted it to.

But honestly, Mom, my sole target audience for this translated version is Radhika. You left a legacy for me and I want to leave it for her in a language that is more accessible to her. Radhika will learn so much in this book about her mother, her *Nani*, and the land of her ancestors, India. She is making good progress in Hindi and I hope she can read the original letters one day. Her children will probably only read the English version. But the words and wisdom you shared with me will continue to flow down from generation to generation.

Mom, this was not an easy project for me. I remember the first day I started working on the translation, I was sitting on a table outside a Starbucks in Redmond. I could not control my tears as I started reading the first letter—it was as if you were speaking to me. After making a big mess of myself in an open-air shopping center and barely having translated a paragraph, I packed my bag and left. It was pretty much the same story day after day, but slowly my heart found the strength to carry on. I made a pledge to complete the project by your birthday in November. Some letters were harder than others to translate. Letters that were more personal, filled with memories from my childhood, were the hardest to get through. Translating your Hindi was not easy either. I had to look up the meaning of many words, message family members, consult with Papa—everyone has been so helpful. At times I had the urge to call you and ask the meaning of a particular word or phrase, or to argue about a certain opinion of yours—only to be reminded of the bitter truth that you are unreachable.

As you have written in one of the letters, we are never alone in our success—our family and friends are partners in our success. This translation project is coming to a successful completion thanks to those partners. Ranveer and Radhika gave me the time and space I needed to work on the translation. I was emotional and often in tears after working through the letters. They wiped my tears and encouraged me to keep going. Papa kept me on my toes by calling every day to ask if the book was finished. Nawin *bhaiya* and Praveen *bhaiya* helped me translate Hindi words and phrases when I got stuck. Sangita *bhabhi*, as always, supported me wholeheartedly. Kalpana *bhabhi* offered to review and edit my translation and put in many hours into making it a better read. She understood how hard this was for me—and it was comforting to have someone share the feeling. My kind friend and neighbor, Heather, showed me the ropes for self-publishing a book. Everyone in the family and my circle of friends cheered me along and shared my belief that this project is worthwhile, and thanks to them, my tribute to you is now complete.

Your Mili
28th October, 2021

Editor's Note

Dear Mili,

May you always be joyful!

First of all, thank you for letting me be a part of this work and helping you with editing. It was an experience that brought me a lot of joy and I was reminded of the times my mother-in-law shared many of the stories written in these letters with me. It also made me miss her more, as I often had a desire to lift the phone and talk with her. Also, following in the vein of this book, I decided to write this as a letter. As my mother-in-law mentioned in one of her letters, writing letters is an important connection with people and the two of us have also exchanged letters by the snail mail.

Did you notice, I said, my mother-in-law and not your mother? My mother-in-law had once told me that when couples talk about their in-laws as "your Mom" it was maintaining a distance in that relationship. An otherness. Saying my mother-in-law is building a closeness in that relationship. Many years ago, I had asked her, "What should I call you? How should I address you?" She said, "This is a great question. When a new daughter-in-law comes to her new home, it is the mother-in-law's job to let her know how to address the people in the new home." I already knew Sangeetaji, your other sister-in-law, called her Mummy. I told my mother-in-law that calling my father-in-law Papa was just fine with me because it did not create any confusion, as I called my own father Daddy. Calling one Daddy and another Papa made it clear who I was talking to or about. But I felt calling her Mummy would be confusing because I would forever be saying things like, *meri* Mummy (my mother) to talk about my birth mother. Which will forever create a distance much like "your Mom". I asked if I should call her *Mataji* as Praveen sometimes refers to her. She said that sounded too heavy. We never really came to a conclusion as to what address I would use for her. Since she was already called Mummy, that is what it ended up being.

When my mother passed away, my mother-in-law wrote a letter to me consoling me and offering to stand in for my mother should I ever need one. The letter touched me deeply and I cherish it to this day. As time went by, and we deepened our bonds as a family, I became more comfortable with calling her Mummy. She too has become *meri* Mummy, as much as *meri* Mummy who gave birth to me.

It is one's good fortune to meet amazing people in this life. Meeting and becoming part of a family with *Srimati* Mridula Sinha was one of them. She was a pioneering woman, who blazed through so many new trails, and broke so many glass ceilings. She worked hard to keep herself grounded and connected with family and friends. She is an inspiration to many, including me.

With love,
Your Kalpana *bhabhi*

—Kalpana Kanwar

A Collection of Letters (Foreword)

We keep telling our children from a very young age, "Do this, do not do that." We feel sad that the children listen at times and ignore our instructions at other times. This is what we think. The truth is that children listen to everything. They absorb what we say in their subconscious mind. They keep it safe like some treasure, and it is evident in how they repeat the same things to their children, in the same accent and form as they heard it from their parents.

In children, girls and boys are different. Girls listen more, they process more. Prominent Hindi writer Mahadevi Verma had said, "If the boys are becoming uncontrollable, let them be. Take care of the daughters. The future of the country will be taken care of. Generations will be saved." Possibly this is why mothers tell more things to their daughters. I, too, told my daughter many things, I told her stories, sang songs to her. But I feel as if a lot was left unsaid. When my daughter left home, my unspoken worries grew. So I started writing letters to her. Then I had a thought, "There are millions of daughters as old as my daughter. They, too, will have daughters. Why not get these letters published? Those millions of daughters should read these too who are out there trying to reach for the stars. No doubt they should reach for the stars. But while keeping their feet on the ground." These letters started getting published monthly in *Swagat* magazine under the title, "Letters to a Daughter Living Abroad."

A lot was left out even after writing so much. If I start writing everything, the book will be very thick. In fact, the process of talking and writing never ends. Letters are a powerful tool of communication. My mother was not educated. She used to make my *chachi* (aunt) write letters to my sister on her behalf. She used to say things in different ways to send her point across. She would not be sure if her emotions were being conveyed by her words. She would say to *chachi*, "You understood it, right? Now write it in your way."

Chachi would read the letter out loud after writing it. Mother would keep making her edits to the letter until it was placed in the mailbox, or the messenger had to leave with the letter for my sister's house. Even after the letter was sent, she would say, "Oh, I forgot to add one thing."

This is from the time when mothers and daughters used to meet after a gap of several years. Now in the age of emails and mobile phones, it feels odd to send hand-written letters. But I don't know why I felt like writing letters to my daughter. After sending her to a foreign country, I had thought of writing only one letter to her. I ended up writing many more. These letters were appreciated by readers who read them in *Swagat* magazine provided to passengers by the Indian Airlines. Passengers would take the magazine home with them to make their daughters read the letters.

This book is a compilation of those letters. The emotions written in the letters are not only for one generation. Our traditions and customs encompass messages from our scriptures and show us the art of living. It is a matter of sadness that our new generation is leaving our traditions behind. The young generation is moving into the cities or going to foreign countries. I am worried that our future generations will be left deprived of the important folk rituals and traditions that nourish life. Therefore, it felt important to publish these letters. It is important to seek societal permission in accepting daughters as special. Generations of daughters will read these letters, will incorporate some parts in their lives. My writing will be successful, and of course, my pen will be blessed. I wish for our daughters to progress on the basis of "old foundation, new construction."

Our daughters can touch the stars, all they need is our trust. These letters ask for trust and confidence in our daughters.

—Mridula Sinha

Contents

A Daughter is Special

My dear daughter Mili,

May you always be happy!

It's your birthday today. You are twenty-five years old now. But you are far away from me at this moment—across seven seas, in another country. Memories from the time of your birth have come alive. You were born after three brothers. The truth is that I was not happy when I learnt that I was pregnant for the fourth time. Your third brother was already six years old. I was thirty-two years old. I was embarrassed as well. But what did my unhappiness and embarrassment have to do with your birth? You were meant for this world. God had chosen my womb for you. This was my destiny and yours. I erased the negative thoughts from my mind and replaced them with happy ones. That happy mind gave rise to a desire. I did not have a daughter. My mother had lamented after the birth of my third son, "My daughter does not have a daughter. After two sons, a girl would have lit up the house with joy."

My mother's wish did not come true in her lifetime. She was already in heaven before you were born. Praveen (your second brother) was already ten years old and Parimal (your youngest brother) was six years old. I overheard their conversation one day. Praveen said, "I wish we get a sister. It will be so much fun!" Parimal said, "Yes *bhaiya* (brother)! And she will tie *rakhis* on us." (Rakhi or Raksha Bandhan is a Hindu festival that celebrates the bond between brothers and sisters.

Sisters tie decorative bracelets (*rakhi*) on their brothers' wrists, and wish for their long, healthy lives.)

Our neighbor, Mrs. Tiwary, used to look at our expansive front yard and say, "I wish you have a daughter. Her wedding would look so beautiful in this yard."

For various reasons, everyone wished for a daughter to be born in my house. R.K. Bahadurji (Ji is an honorific added to names.) used to live in the lower level of our house. When it was time to deliver you, his twenty-five-year-old son was the one who drove me to the hospital. On the way, he would point to cows, goats, and every female animal he could spot and keep saying to me, "Aunty, look at this one. This is good omen. You will certainly have a daughter!"

It was the day of Chhath festival. (Chhath is celebrated six days after Diwali. People pray to the Sun God on this day.) You were born shortly after 3:00 in the early hours of the day. Your *chachi* (father's brother's wife) and Prabha *phua* (father's sister) were in the hospital room with me, waiting for the nurse to reveal the gender. As soon as the nurse said, "it's a girl," your Prabha *phua* jumped with excitement and exclaimed, "Congratulations, *bhabhi* (sister-in-law)! It's a girl! It's a girl!"

Through the loudspeakers we could hear the refrains of the Chhath festival songs being sung at the riverbanks, "God, grant me a daughter to help distribute the sweet offerings of this prayer." We could hear the bursts of fireworks. It was the night of the Chhath fast. The devotees were waiting for the sun to rise. My wait was already over. My daughter was already here.

I too was happy. I had forgotten all my pains. The absence of a daughter in my life was now no more. The happiness one feels after getting a thing or a person is a measure of its lack. If I already had a daughter, I may not have welcomed you with the same joy. Sons and daughters are both important. If you have a son, you wish for a daughter. If you have a daughter, you wish for a son. When you have one son and one daughter, they say a family is complete.

It is hard to describe in words how it felt to have you in my life. You were growing at the speed of a waxing moon. You were ten months old on your first Rakhi. Your brothers were thrilled beyond words. Their sister was going to tie *rakhis* on their wrists for the first time. All three brothers showered and dressed in their best clothes and lined up happily for the occasion. Parimal's face was lit with joy. It was a joyful scene to behold. It was festive. A festival that celebrates the special bond between sisters and brothers. The only person who was unaware of the happiness of the festivities was you. We got to celebrate that day because of you but you were oblivious. We placed the platter with *rakhis* and sweets in front of you, and you immediately picked up a *rakhi* and put it in your mouth. Parimal shouted, "No, Mili, don't put it in your mouth. We have to do the prayers."

The three brothers touched the *rakhis* to your hands and tied them on their own wrists. They could not stop admiring how beautiful their *rakhi*-adorned wrists looked. You were toddling around in your frilly dress and tinkling anklets. The brothers' wish had come true. Since your arrival, our home had a completely different feel to it. Anyone who came by would only talk about your activities. Mili does this, Mili does that! You achieved all milestones fast—as if you were in a rush to grow up. In fact, I was the one who was in a rush. In the midst of the joy of raising you, sometimes this thought would cross my mind, "How long will I be able to raise her? I am growing older. Her education, wedding, etc., are all yet to be taken care of."

It was as if you could read my thoughts. That's why you reached your milestones faster than your brothers did. Turning over at three months, sitting up and getting your first teeth at four months, and walking at seven months. You also started understanding your elders' emotions at a very young age. God gives special skills to daughters. They are more sensitive to others' emotions. You were merely six years old. The year you were born was when your third brother was diagnosed with an illness. Overtime, his muscles grew weak and he could not move by himself. He became dependent on others for even the simplest of tasks. You took special care of him. And he of you. I was broken up inside by that child's illness, but I tried very consciously to appear outwardly calm. It was not right to make his surroundings sad. I was also worried for you. I got you after many prayers. I tried to be happy so that I did not burden your childhood. One day you asked me, "Mom, why don't you laugh like other mothers do? Why are you sad?"

I forced a smile on my face and said, "No, my dear. I laugh a lot." Sensing my pretense, you said, "Okay listen, I know you cry for Parimal *bhaiya*. I am telling you he will get better. During my school prayers, I pray every day for God to make him better. He will be alright. You should laugh more."

I kept trying to stay happy for your sake. Despite your prayers, your brother did not get well. He left us. When I look back at the eleven years he spent with you, I realize that you gave him everything—love, company, care, and your motherly touch. Yes, your little palms had motherly love. Your brother found your touch healing. That's why he ignored the nurse by his side and would call for you, "Mili! Mili!".

You used to leave your homework and run to him. You never ignored his call for help. You would come up to him and say, "What is it now? I still have to finish my Hindi and math homework. I also need to go play. Tell me what you need!" Your complaints were all very motherly. Your brother would smile, "Can you flip the page of this book for me?" Sometimes he said, "Bend my legs." You would quickly help him out and run off to finish your homework. He called you every ten minutes. He was born with a genetic disorder. But the symptoms began showing up only after you were born.

Not just your brother! I had major surgery when you were eight years old. While discharging me, the doctors had instructed, "Do not bend or lift anything during bath time." You heard the instructions. And that was it. You would not let me enter the bathroom on my own. You helped me bathe. I still remember the feel of your little hands on my body helping me bathe. Those memories give me strength. Your touch was healing. I didn't need to make you bathe me, clothe me, or brush my hair. But I was hoping it would give you the training and practice in taking care of others. And of course, it made me happy too.

One day you said to me in a worried tone, "Mom, I will have to do so much work when I grow up. Cooking, teaching the kids, entertaining guests, writing stories, and giving speeches. Goodness, how will I manage all the work?"

Someone commented, "There will also be a husband. What will he do?"

"He will read the newspaper, talk to people, shave, and go to work," you replied.

This incident showed me that you had a sense of responsibility at a very young age. This is called "*sanskaar*" (values). I believe that children learn better by observing their parents rather than listening to their instructions. I was not able to visit your school often. Once I visited your kindergarten classroom and your teacher was very happy to see me. She said, "Your daughter is very *sanskaari*. How do you teach her everything?" I said, "she is your student. I am sure you are the one who is teaching her." Your teacher was full of praise for you and I was reminded of the lines by the poet Kabir: "When a parent and teacher are both present, who should I pay respects to first? The parent says first bow to the teacher!"

People are realizing today that the cooperation of parents and teachers is very important for the development of children. The culture of the schools and families need to be similar. To help children grow, both parties work together to fill a need. Whenever I hear parents blame teachers for their children's failure in front of the children, or hear teachers criticize parents in front of their children, I get annoyed. At that tender age, you had more respect for your teacher than you had for me. You heard your teachers and parents admiring each other and that led you to have good *sanskaar*.

You moved up the classes with good grades. You always made us happy. Twenty-five years have gone by. I would not have let you go to another country at such a young age had I not known that you have the ability to take care of yourself and to understand people. You had maturity from a young age. I believed that even in another country, you would spread the scent of the familial-social values of our country. You would share the special qualities of Indian family life with students from other countries. Your presence in another country is serving that purpose too, so I am happy to have sent you.

I am certainly sad to not be with you on your birthday. Until you were ten years old, you insisted on having a cake to cut and candles to blow out but I did not allow it. We did celebrate your birthday. We invited your friends over for sweets and cake. We lit diyas (earthen lamps), but never blew them out. Eventually your friends understood. Birthdays can be celebrated without blowing out candles. That's how it should be. I trust that even today when you celebrate your birthday in Ithaca (a town in New York), you will not be lighting and blowing out twenty-five candles. You will explain to your friends, "In Indian culture, we do not blow out lit candles. We believe a lit lamp represents life. So why would we want to snuff it out? It is considered bad omen to blow out candles."

Your friends from America, China, Japan, Germany, and other countries will definitely understand. This is how a culture grows and stays alive. It is our responsibility to teach our children to respect our culture and traditions and explain the significance of the traditions to them. Girls in your generation seem eager to learn the significance of Indian traditional rituals. That is a positive sign. This is why the Indian culture has been thriving for thousands of years. And will continue to thrive.

Everyone who had wished for your birth for numerous reasons has had their wish fulfilled. Brothers got a sister, father got a daughter, and other relatives also felt happy. Our neighbor Mrs. Tiwari is no longer alive. But before you were born, she wished for your wedding to take place in our front yard. Now the time has come for us to receive your groom.

Finding a good match for daughters and getting them married is indeed a hard job, but also pleasurable. I now realize that for many reasons, sons and daughters are not the same. Daughters are special. I am happy to be the mother of a special child—a child who gives joy, gives peace, one whose company is soothing.

Your Mom

□

Sons and Daughters: Not Equals

My darling daughter Mili,

Good wishes!

You have suddenly grown up; I did not even realize. It feels as if you were born yesterday. As if I just looked up after sewing buttons onto a tiny dress I made for you, and as I reached to put the dress on you I had to keep raising my eyes. My eyes had to travel up five feet and three inches to see all of you. You were standing in front of me wearing a white *kurta* in Lucknow embroidery, adjusting your long scarf, and announcing to me, "Mom, I have received an acceptance letter from Cornell University in the New York state of America. They will give me $20,000 per year in assistantship, on top of full coverage of tuition fees. I too will go to America just like *bhaiya* (elder brother) did. I want to continue higher studies after my master's. Mom, please don't stop me. Let me go."

You were shaking me gently to rouse me from my daze. You were all grown up now and you were making life decisions on your own. I had not realized. But what does my realization have to do with anything? Of course, you were twenty-two years old!

I had to make the decision to separate you from myself. It is not uncommon for girls your age to get separated from their parents, leave for their in-laws' house. I got married when I was sixteen years old. My mother was married at the age of twelve. I heard that my grandmother was married off when she was five years old. She just slept in her mother's arms during the wedding ceremony. It is time to start thinking about your wedding. It is one thing to send a daughter of this age away after getting her married. It was not easy for me to harden my heart to send you away at a marriageable age without getting you married, that too to another country. You could sense my emotions when you said, "Mom, one day I have to leave your house. That is the custom. You had to leave your mother too, right?" You continued, "And you sent *bhaiya* away ten years ago. If you can stay without him, why not without me?"

In that moment, I started thinking of the difference between a son and a daughter. In fact, in my opinion, sons and daughter are not equal in many respects. It is one thing to send a son to another country and another to send a daughter. When you were born, I had realized that I will have to take special care of you, I will have to worry more about you than I do for my sons. And I did. Nature has created girls to be different from boys, and for this reason, sons can live their lives more freely, go anywhere unaccompanied, but not daughters. Raising daughters in a different manner than sons, taking into account the difference in their physical composition, does not mean daughters are discriminated against. Those who raise daughters and sons the same way are mistaken. Nature has created girls in a special way, and therefore they need to be raised and provided for in a special way. Daughters become mothers, sons do not.

Sons and daughters are different in one more way. Mahadevi Verma had once said, "When a son takes a wrong turn in life, people say he has become *awara* (a vagrant). A daughter is never called *awara*. The society does not expect a daughter to become a vagrant."

Another difference between a son and a daughter is that a daughter is always a giver. She gives birth as a mother, gives support as a sister, and gives love, confidence, and companionship to her husband as a wife. Just like a giver's hand is raised, a woman's place in society is also higher than a man's. For this reason, a woman should not be treated as a man's equal, but with more respect. Women have special responsibilities towards the society, so the opportunities provided to them need to be special too, not just equal.

During the times in history that are considered the dark ages for society, when women had not progressed, men may not have been very educated but they knew how to respect women. Women were transported from one place to another on the shoulders of men. A woman, whether she was an eight-year-old girl (married) or a sixty-year-old lady, had to be carried on the shoulders of four men in a *doli* (palanquin). If the woman was attacked, the four men would risk their lives to fight for her honor. This was a symbol of society's respect for a woman. It has been considered the society's responsibility to provide safety and respect to women in different walks of life. A woman is society's treasure, for society to protect.

Where am I wandering! You used to always get mad at me for getting lost in my thoughts. You reminded me, "Mom, now don't give me a lecture. Tell me, what should I do?"

It was your habit from childhood to tell me all your goings-on in detail—where you went, who you met. It is a fact that a daughter becomes a mother's friend when she grows up. They share everything. It is very important to have this openness between moms and daughters. I did not always teach you, I also learnt from you. I have taken your suggestions. We may be three decades apart in our ages, but we are very close because of our openness. This openness had led to a trust—a bond of trust we have nurtured with honest effort.

What should I say to a daughter asking for permission to go to another country?

This was a big question. I was not over sending my son away ten years earlier for higher education in America. He had insisted. We had made him promise that he will return tc his motherland, India. India is a very beautiful country. There may not be a lot of money here, but there is a lot of affection. The smell of your motherland's soil is always sweet. Our son had reassured us that he would return after completing his higher studies abroad. It felt as if he left a hole in my heart when he left. Your question about leaving raised so many questions in my mind. Many different emotions were rising up in my heart.

There was another problem. We had become more dependent on you. Your dad had come to rely on you for many things. He found talking to you enjoyable and calming. He would often ask you for help. You too had begun to care for his daily needs without any prompting from me. Daughters understand their fathers well from a very young age. Fathers are usually more dependent on their daughters. You also helped me brainstorm and troubleshoot my problems. It was not going to be easy to let you go.

I knew though that I had to let you go. How would a girl who had not spent a single night away from home in twenty-two years of her life, live in an unfamiliar country amongst unknown people? How will she take to the new foods and customs she is not used to? Your own country is your own, it's your home and you can live here freely. In a foreign country you are a foreigner. You will be treated differently, always seen as an outsider. To be always othered is also a difficult thing to bear.

Forget all these problems, whatever happens, will happen. After all, thousands of Indian students live in America, why couldn't you? You left. Since you are there, it is my duty to caution you on some important points. I am confident you will give careful consideration to these points.

First, even in a foreign land, you will meet some people who will offer you help and others who will seek your help. It will be a test of your wisdom to distinguish between them. Be vigilant about whose help to take and who to help. Take every step carefully. Nature has given you special powers as a girl to recognize and understand people.

It is a foreign nation, foreign people. However, it is not difficult to win over foreign hearts. Sometimes they may become closer to you than your own kind. I hope you will not forget to appreciate their lifestyle, food, and their friendliness.

It is important to stay proud of your culture, your traditions, your food, your lifestyle. I have sowed those seeds in you. Being proud of your heritage does not imply that another's heritage is not praiseworthy. It is good to compare, but never good to criticize another's culture.

That's all for today. You are physically across the seven seas, but not far from my heart. I will keep writing about thoughts and advice that come to my mind, not just for you, but for so many other Indian girls who have gone abroad. Consider these as your mother's advice, not lectures. My dear, keep practicing what I have taught you so far in life.

Your Mom

□

Daughter's Gift

My dear Mili,

Always stay happy!

So, we have been seeking several prospective grooms for you lately. We did not take out a matrimonial ad in the newspapers, just using word of mouth amongst our close friends and family. We have made a long list. After inquiring about the details of eligible bachelors, we also tell them about the fine qualities of our family. We also tell them that we have not raised our daughter in luxury. She has grown up lacking many comforts.

You may not remember, but I will never forget this incident. You were in the seventh grade. You kept asking for a bicycle. I kept listening and kept reassuring you that I would buy it next month. Maybe you were disappointed with my procrastination, so you went ahead and also asked your father. He immediately handed Rs. 600 out of his wallet to me and said, "Buy my daughter a bicycle." Two more months passed by in waiting and you complained to your father, "Mom didn't buy the bicycle." You father asked me, "Why! I gave you money for it. Why didn't you buy the bicycle?

I calmly presented my well-thought-out response, "Our daughter should realize that even a bicycle is a big thing and that not all wants in life can be fulfilled immediately." You probably did not understand the meaning of my words, but your father did. He bought his first pair of tailored dress pants when he began his undergraduate studies in college, and they were his only dress pants until he graduated.

There is one piece of sad news. Your friend Sonia got divorced. Divorce is not new to our society. It has always been acceptable in the extreme classes—the very rich and the very poor. These days divorce is becoming common even among the middle class. There are many causes for this, but I think the most important reason is the mismatch between families. These sorts of marriages are also not uncommon in our society. These mismatched marriages have happened all along. It is an unmatched pair if the boy and girl are too dissimilar in age, appearance, or ability. But these days many marriages are happening despite a mismatch between the two families—mismatch in economic status of the families, or mismatch in family values and *sanskaars* (culture; values).

Sonia has not experienced want in her life. Even before she was born, her big room had a big closet overflowing with toys. Her room was decorated with anything and everything a child can ask for. As she grew, so did the number of toys she owned. In fact, Sonia never needed to ask for anything.

When she began preschool, her nanny dropped her off in a shiny new car. During the course of her three years of college with you, her personal cars got upgraded six or seven times. The boy her father found for her marriage was an I.A.S. (an officer in the Indian Administrative Services). The son of a schoolteacher, an eligible bachelor. Just think! How would they get along? One grew up lacking many comforts of life, the other grew up wrapped in luxuries and coddled.

Sonia's mother was visiting. With tearful eyes, she said, "*Bahenji* (sister), I spent one crore (ten million) Rupees on my daughter's wedding. It was a lavish wedding. What gift didn't I give her? Even then her marriage didn't last."

What could I say? I did ask, "*Bahenji*. Did you give your daughter a wedding or make a business deal with her in-laws?"

"Of course I gave her a wedding. Why would I do a business deal?" she replied irritably.

I tried to explain, "*Bahenji*, you started describing the wedding with the mention of one crore Rupees."

I asked Sonia, "*Beti* (daughter), did you ever wake up early to make tea for your parents-in-law?" She gave a quick reply, "No, aunty. There was no shortage of helpers in our house. Even Mom had sent three helpers with me at the time of the wedding. My husband's house already had two helpers. Why would I need to make tea for my parents-in-law? Plus, I woke up at 9 a.m. and I heard they had their morning tea at 5 a.m.!"

Little things in life lead to big things. Small milestones help cover a long distance. On one hand, Sonia's husband Rakesh could not distance himself from the life of restrictions he was used to with his school-teacher father. On the other hand, what is Sonia's fault? She was born with a silver spoon in her mouth. It is neither the boy's nor the girl's fault, but there was a problem.

There was a problem. Two unmatched families got into a relationship. The relation between the father of the groom and the father of the bride is known as "*samdhi.*" "*Sam*" means similar in Hindi; the two fathers should have similar cultures and living conditions. In our culture, people also match the *kundalis* (horoscopes) of the prospective bride and groom. The tradition continues today even among modern families. I believe in matching the *kundalis* of not just the bride and groom, but also their families. Mismatched marriages have always been happening in society, but earlier people used to exercise patience in keeping the relationship going. Today, people neither have the patience nor the time for tolerance.

We received the biodata of a boy for you. He is doing research at an American university, just like you. His family is ultra-modern. For three generations his family members have served as high-level government officials. His father is retired. All their relatives either live in big cities or abroad. I have been thinking whether or not to send your marriage proposal to them. Because we are a middle-class family. We are still closely associated with rural life and the poor. Part of the wedding ceremonies also involves a meeting of the relatives. These relationships fare well if they are more equal.

We are also thinking of these things when trying to select a groom for you. The ultimate decision is yours to make. The fact of the matter is that despite the disparities in family backgrounds, a number of these marriages appear to be happy and content. No one rule applies when it comes to marriages.

A friend reached out to me, "There is a very good boy. He has done engineering and management. He works at a good company. His parents are asking for 10 lakh (1 million) Rupees."

"I don't want my daughter married into that kind of family," I said to her.

All our lives we keep gifting our daughters something or the other. But I cannot marry my daughter into a family that is greedy for gifts and asks for dowry. There is no end to asking for dowry. The more they get, the more they want. Trying to please people who ask for dowry is like adding *ghee* (fats) to the (ceremonial) fire, it only makes the fire burn stronger and longer.

What are the poor parents to do when their own daughters ask for dowry? These days very few girls want to get married without dowry. They too want to experience the joys of life, all the creature comforts. They start complaining if their parents don't give dowry at the time of their wedding. They want the lavish weddings as shown in the movies. Late Mrs. Mahadevi Verma had said, "Many girls are torched these days when parents give no dowry. I am looking for hundred girls who are willing to marry with no dowry. I can bring a revolution in society with the support of those hundred girls. I haven't found even ten girls yet, let alone hundred." That was a different time. Mahadevi Verma is now no more. I believe we can find those girls if we look again in these times.

I have not saved much for your wedding. Why should I give whatever I have saved from my earnings to only your brothers? I would like to give something to you as well if you need it.

You may remember when your elder brothers got married, I did not ask for dowry for both my sons. We found a match for our first son, the second one found his own. We made sure the two families' cultures matched at the time of Nawin's wedding. Our lifestyles were similar. We did not display the gifts our daughter-in-law got from her parents; we did not even see them ourselves. The gifts were for their daughter. We also did not see and evaluate the girl before the wedding. How could I? To see a girl and then reject her for her looks is an inhuman act in my view.

I could not do that. I have never found a girl ugly. When you do not receive the gift of beauty from God, you surely get some other great qualities that outweigh your looks. There was something I liked very much about your *bhabhi* (sister-in-law) Sangita's family. It was one of the main factors for accepting their marriage proposal. The two elderly women who lived in the small apartment on the ground floor of your to-be *bhabhi's* home were her *dadi* (paternal grandmother) and *nani* (maternal grandmother). They all lived together. My *bhatiji* (paternal niece) Kiran knew the family well. She had told me that the two elderly ladies lived happily. That gave me an indication of their family's culture. The children of the house must also know how to respect and care for the elderly.

Then, I had to get a son married. Now, it is my daughter. I wonder at what stage of the human civilization a bride's family's hand came below (of lower status) the groom's. Gift of a daughter is known as *"kanyadaan."* But a giver's hand is always on the top, isn't' it? Then why is it expected for a family who gifts their daughter to also act in a deferential manner? It is a matter for social research. In our society, a groom is treated like a king. Daughters are called Laxmi (a symbol of prosperity). Daughters are spoken to respectfully. Even after the birth of a third or fourth daughter in a family, people say jokingly, "Laxmi is here." Of course, daughters are Laxmis. Kunwar Bechain, a Hindi poet has said, "Daughters are a cool breeze." Truth! A daughter's presence does feel like the brush of a cool breeze. It brings serenity and peace to our souls.

In our unique culture, a son-in-law is considered an incarnation of Vishnu and respected accordingly. It is best to enter into a bond of marriage after matching the qualities of the two families.

More some other time...
Your Mom

□

The Companionship of a Mother-in-Law (*Saas*)

Darling daughter Mili,

Blessings!

We came across a prospective groom who seemed like a good match for you in every way. However, people who know the family say that his mother has a short temper. They also remarked, "How does it matter for your daughter? It's not like she has to live with her *saas* (mother-in-law). She will live in America. The boy is a gem, so what if his mother has a bad temper?"

This shook me to my core. I thought, "How is this possible? This would imply that even before your marriage I should assume that either you will be deprived of your mother-in-law's affection or your mother-in-law of your love and care."

I do not consider this a happy outcome. I believe that relationships help human lives become happy and successful. In this regard I consider a mother-in-law to be another mother. Maybe even above a mother. Our society has wonderful mothers-in-law, or should I say mothers-in-law who are mothers, friends, and supporters of their *bahus* (daughters-in-law). In our social culture, people have been sowing seeds of fear about mothers-in-law in girls' minds. This is not right in any way. Just like any relationship can be good or bad, so can the relationship between a *saas* and a *bahu*. Then why defame the *saas*?

It is natural for the *saas-bahu* relationship to be bittersweet. After the birth of a son, a mother dedicates herself to raising him with no thoughts to her own comforts. She diligently raises him. When the son is of marriageable age, she starts dreaming of bringing home her *bahu*. If her twenty-five-year-old son tells her, "Mom, now you live your own life. Let us live our lives," then the fifty-year-old mother will start looking for her life. Where is her life? She let it go twenty-five years ago. Sleeping when the son slept, waking when he awoke. Raising him with hopes of making him a worthy person. So is there anything left of her own life? It is no wonder that even the distance created by the seven seas cannot distance a mother from her son and daughter-in-law. She should not have to.

During the initial days of a marriage, there are conflicts between the *saas* and the *bahu* because of differences in their family culture and traditions. The mother-in-law wants her daughter-in-law to adapt to the ways she has been running her household for twenty-five years. The wise ones give their daughters-in-law time to adapt, while the less patient ones insist they change their ways sooner. Wise mothers-in-law are able to hide the emotion of having lost control over their sons; others are not able to. That is the only difference.

In the situation of a conflict, both have to make an effort to reconciliate. It is expected for the mother-in-law to make a greater effort to get along because she is not only older and more experienced, but she is also in her home ground. The daughter-in-law comes from another house. A mother-in-law plays an important role in helping the daughter-in-law understand and adapt to the ways of the family.

Your Vimla aunty has a step-mother-in-law. I cannot explain the depth of love and understanding in their relationship. Vimla's mother-in-law is the one who raised both her kids. Now she is raising Vimla's grandson too. It must be difficult caring for her great grandson at her age, but she never complains. Her daughter-in-law Vimla works as a professor and Vimla's daughter-in-law has a corporate job.

Vimla's daughter-in-law comes from a very different kind of family, but on observing her grandmother-in-law's wisdom and large heartedness, she remarks, "I want to grow up to be like grandma."

How wise is this modern daughter-in-law of the new generation! How much trust she has in the older generation! This trust is earned by both sides.

Last year I traveled to America. An Indian woman, also from Bihar (a state in India), lives there. She brought her sick mother-in-law from Bihar to live with her. She quit her job to take care of her mother-in-law.

Your grandmother, my mother-in-law, used to say to me during the early days of my marriage, "You are a wild bird we have brought into our house. Our house is the bird cage you have to live in. We will have to lovingly teach you how to speak the human language. And that job is mine." By "human language" she meant the norms and culture of the household.

I know of several women who forget their own mothers after being with their mothers-in-law. They hold their mothers-in-law closer to their hearts than their mothers. Girls who get nice mothers-in-law are considered lucky because a good relationship between the two is the basis for a happy household.

Two years ago, your sister-in-law was expecting a child. She was in America and I was in India. The thought that she was cooking for herself in that condition used to trouble me. I did not wait for an invitation to go be with her. I felt a sense of satisfaction after cooking and feeding her various delicacies for a week. I felt labor pains along with both my daughters-in-law during the time of their deliveries. This was my way of paying back for my mother-in-law's good behavior towards me. Behaving nicely with my daughters-in-law, just like she did with me, is indeed like returning the favor.

You are my only daughter. But I do not see any difference between you and my daughters-in-law. You get the love and care not only from your mother, but also from your sisters-in-law. I will take some credit for establishing this sort of a relationship between you and them.

Life is short. People have been adding color and meaning to their lives by nurturing sweet and strong relationships. It is true that we expect different things from each relationship. However, it is also true that a person who is able to maintain good relationships is said to have led a successful life. A life to emulate. In my opinion, life means getting along. Movies and literature have to take some blame for souring the relationship between mothers-in-law and daughters-in-law. Even literature written with the aim of nurturing the relationship often misses the mark.

Many mothers- and sisters-in-law are incarcerated in our society for torturing daughters-in-law for dowry. On seeing young girls behind bars in Delhi's Tihar Jail, I asked, "What crimes have they committed?" "Assisting their mothers in torturing or burning their sisters-in-law," I was told.

Laws were made to protect the newly-wed girls in their in-laws' house from dowry-related crimes. When the laws were strictly enforced, many mothers- and sisters-in-law started getting incarcerated. A fear of law is also required to make these relationships smooth and simple. However, relationships cannot thrive on the basis of fear. Threats do not build close relationships. They are nurtured with love. You invest in each other to earn the rights to the other's love and care. I often ask the newly-wed girls, "Do you make tea for your mother-in-law first thing in the morning?"

I suggest this because even if for some reason the mother- and daughter-in-law had a small conflict the night before, when the mother-in-law sees her daughter-in-law offering her a cup of tea in the morning, then any remaining resentment will disappear just like the steam rising from the cup of tea. In my times, when a girl departed for her in-laws' after the wedding, she was advised "As soon as you wake up, pay respects to your mother-in-law. Massage her feet every night when she goes to bed." These two acts were meant as gestures to keep the mothers-in-law happy and strengthen the bond between them. Just think, our elders who we call uneducated were so wise at understanding human psychology. Nowadays in nuclear families, mothers- and daughters-in-law do not live together. Living together can cause friction. However, physical distance can also widen the distance between the hearts because people cannot love and care for each other.

This happens in all relationships, not just between mothers-in-law and daughters-in-law. When a new bride visits her maternal home for the first time, she is often asked, "How is your mother-in-law?" Her family wants to make sure the mother-in-law is good-hearted so that their daughter's life is smooth.

My mother had asked me the same question when I visited home three days after my wedding. I blurted out, "Nicer than you."

This abrupt answer could have troubled my mother. But instead, she was thrilled. She was satisfied. She never asked me again about my mother-in-law. She was reassured of my place in my in-laws' house. That was enough for her.

Our lives are woven with the warp and woof of relationships. They each add their own color and flavor to our lives.

These days the trend is to live your own life. It is considered a modern practice even for husbands and wives to live their own individual lives. This trend will soon become old-fashioned too. After thousands of years of experimentation and examination of family life, one factor that has stood out is that living for others brings happiness. This is the foundation of a family life in our culture. One family member's right is hidden in another's duty. Everyone in the family is aware of this unwritten constitution of family life. To find happiness in serving others is also a selfish act. A life lived for oneself becomes a burden. Therefore, a married life is considered to be the best life. You are living in America as a student. You save whatever little you can and bring presents for your nieces and other family members every time you visit. This act of giving gives you happiness.

You were very little. You were studying. Your brother came home from outside. I asked you to make tea for him.

You said, "Mom, even for you a son and daughter are not the same. Your son has come back after playing. You asked your daughter who was studying to get up and make tea for him."

I did not explain at that time. You made tea and brought it. Everyone praised your tea. After some time I said, "Mili, you were studying for quite a while. You made tea on my request. Everyone praised it. You also felt happy. By doing small things for others we gain a lot of happiness. We can also become more engaged in our work."

This was all part of your training. That is why even in America you cook Indian food for your many friends every now and then. It most certainly gives you pleasure.

Here in our house, you used to help everyone without being asked to. You even enjoyed helping out our house maid with her work. Doing dishes in the kitchen, sweeping the floors, folding laundry—you would do everything without anyone asking. In return you got the love and respect of everyone in the house.

Receiving and distributing this happiness is only possible in a family. Sometimes it is possible to maintain these relationships even from a distance. People often grow apart even while staying under the same roof. That is why when finding a marriage prospect for you, we have to consider not only the boy but also the temperament and behavior of his family.

It is wonderful that nowadays even people living in nuclear families have started recognizing the importance of a joint family. Understanding this is sufficient.

So far, none of the marriage prospects for you have gelled. I will keep looking.

Your Mom

□

Sati Savitri
(Faithful and Devoted Savitri)

My beloved Mili,

Blessings!

These days I am looking for a suitable husband and family for you. That is why I keep pondering over many factors related to matchmaking. It is not a new tradition in our country for a girl to find her own match. This type of wedding, where the girl chooses her groom is called *svayamvar* (husband found by self) and it is one of the eight types of weddings accepted in Hindu scriptures. It is also a shocking fact that in our culture the right to choose a partner was only given to girls, not to boys. This implies that the society expected girls to have the discretion and the wisdom needed to understand the gravity of marriage.

However, when parents become matchmakers, they need to consider a whole host of things—ages of the two individuals, the socio-economic status of the two families, the *janma-patri's* (the alignment of the stars), religion and sect, etc. In fact, this process of matchmaking based on matching *janma-patri's*, religion, etc., does not seem old-fashioned at all. These days a scientific approach to matchmaking also involves consideration of the same factors that were determined to be key for matchmaking by Indian saints, intellectuals, and social researchers.

In this context, I am often reminded of the ancient story of Sati Savitri. It is sad that these days girls are not raised on the stories of *pati-vrata* (a wife devoted to her husband) women such as Sati Savitri, Sita, Anusuya, Draupadi, and Mandodari. Their stories are neither being taught at school, nor at home. Girls are not told the importance of a woman being *pati-vrata*. As if being *pati-vrata* is a matter of crime or backwardness, a pretense. If you call a woman *pati-vrata*, she might get offended thinking you are making fun of her. But I have always been fascinated by the story of Sati Savitri. To me, Savitri was a character beyond her time. In my opinion, parents should present Savitri as a role model for their daughters and feel proud of their daughters if they turn out like her. Now let me tell you the story of Savitri and Satyavaan in short. I will then explain the significance of this story which I treasure.

Savitri was the brilliant daughter of the famous and saintly king of Madra-desh, King Ashwapati. She was of marriageable age. As word of her brilliance and intelligence spread, no one dared to approach the king for her hand, nor was the king able to find a match for her. The king was worried and told his daughter, "I will arrange for a carriage, a general, horses, and helpers. Search the *ashrams* (hermitages) and travel the lands to find a suitable match for yourself."

Savitri followed her father's orders. After completing the search for her groom, she returned and informed the king, "When the saintly King Ghamratsen of Shalv-desh lost his eyesight, the neighboring king attacked and acquired his kingdom. King Ghamratsen went to live in the forest with his wife and baby. His son was raised in the forest. That talented boy Satyavaan is a suitable match for me. I have decided to marry him."

It so happened that Saint Naarad was present when Savitri said this. He said, "Satyavaan has a very short life." The King requested his daughter to change her decision, but she did not agree. She was a *Sati*, already devoted to Satyavaan. She said, "Father, division of wealth, giving a daughter's hand in marriage, or accepting someone as a husband only happens once. Now I cannot accept anyone other than Satyavaan as my husband."

Savitri and Satyavaan had a grand wedding. She went to live in the forest with her husband. One day Satyavaan headed out into the forest to collect wood and fruits. Savitri also went along with him. All of a sudden, Satyavaan felt dizzy and he lay his head down in Savitri's lap to rest. He died right away. According to the scriptures, the Lord of Death, Yamraj, himself came to collect his soul. Savitri started following Yamraj. Yamraj said, "You should return home and perform the last rites for your husband." But Savitri kept following Yamraj.

Pleased with his conversation with Savitri , Yamraj granted her a wish. Savitri asked for the return of her father-in-law's eyesight, a son for her father, and for her father-in-law's kingdom to be restored to him. Yamraj kept saying, "so be it," and granted all her wishes. In the end, Savitri asked, "Lord, I wish for a hundred sons to expand my family."

Yamraj said, "So be it. Surely you can go back now?" Savitri said, "Walking with my husband is not making me feel tired, nor sad. On the contrary, I am fortunate to have the noble company of a great man like you. Now if you could please return Satyavaan's life, only then you will be able to keep your word to me. I desire nothing for my life other than my husband, and without him, your granted wish of a hundred sons for me will not come to fruition." Impressed by Savitri's piousness and intelligence, Yamraj returned Satyavaan's life.

This story shows how pious and brilliant women of India were at that time. They were not helpless. To save her husband's life, Savitri did not beg. She argued with Yamraj intelligently and defeated him. We have many such women in our history, whose personalities are not weaker than men. In every society, there are stories of such ideal men and women; stories that are repeated as part of religious festivities for the benefit of the younger generations. This way some of the qualities of these role models are retained in the future generations, and the historical characters are kept alive amongst us, as well as our life ideals.

These days, in order to provide protection from diseases such as AIDS, people are encouraged to be monogamous. I believe that our Indian thinkers and saints must have come up with the mantra of "one-wife vow" after a detailed study and research of human and social science. That became an ideology. In the name of being progressive, one cannot leave behind everything old. In the name of individualism, we left our ideologies and gave rise to carelessness. Now we are suffering the consequences. In our culture, the values of life have been propagated by way of various festivals, religious functions, and rituals. Every individual carries these values in their blood. This is why this *sanskriti* (culture) cannot be stopped, it will stay alive.

There is another aspect of Savitri's story which also applies to you. Savitri was so bright and intelligent that no prince dared to come ask for her in marriage. The king got worried and asked his daughter to go travel the country and find a groom on her own.

When people suggest a prospective groom for you, the first thing they mention is, "The boy earns well. He will be wealthy."

It is true that these days everyone looks for a prospect who earns well—not just the girls' parents but the girls themselves too. However, when Savitri was asked to find herself a groom, she found someone who came from a saint family. The son of a king who lived in a forest. But Satyavaan's qualities matched well with those of Savitri's. It is important to note that Savitri was herself a great evaluator of human personalities, and that is how she was able to recognize Satyavaan's qualities. She did not nag to get her husband back. Yamraj was impressed by her intelligent and practical arguments about life and the world, and he kept granting her one wish after another. In the end she was able to win her husband back because of her eloquence. That is how she joined the ranks of *pati-vrata* (devoted to her husband) women.

In the name of independence, girls and boys cannot be carefree. Carefree relationships are baseless and empty, and therefore do not bring pleasure.

Reading this letter, you must be getting mad at me about now. If you were here, you would have said, "That's enough, Mom. Tell me if you found someone for me already."

I have already said, you too should look for a match. I am searching too. I know you are not in a hurry. You will not agree to marry someone just on emotional grounds. These very qualities of yours make it hard for us to find a match for you.

There was another reason to tell you the story of Sati Savitri—that you understand the true meaning of *pati-vrata*. That you develop respect for women who are *pati-vrata*. Being progressive should be an aspect of life for you, not just a trendy thing to do. These women hidden in the pages of our history books and scriptures are role models for girls living modern lives. Women who were self-made, worked on making their mind and body strong. Prepared themselves to live life. These types of women are able to make a commitment to their husbands, the society, and the world. Any work done with commitment and honesty serves as a fulfillment of your duties.

Fulfilling your duties as a wife is being a *pati-vrata*. In the self-actualization of girls, the rule should be "old foundation, new construction." No society develops its ideologies in one day. Those women are a part of your foundation. You have to think how you want to learn and adopt their various qualities. How you want to build yourself.

Next month there will be Vat-Savitri festivities in different parts of the country. Married women will sit under a banyan tree and listen to the story of Savitri and Satyavaan. They will offer prayers to the banyan trees. Those who don't have banyan trees around their house will plant one when the rains come. Think, how many different aspects of one festival! This is how those trees as well as Savitri and Satyavaan are alive amongst us. As long as there is life and society, there will be ideologies meant to keeping the environment clean, marriages stable, and husbands and wives devoted to each other completely. This is how it should be. I hope you will tell this story to your friends in America, even the boys. They have to become qualified and illustrious like Satyavaan so that they can find wives like Savitri. Partners in good and bad times. Willing to sacrifice their lives for each other.

Your Mom

□

Pleasures of a Joint Family

Dear Mili,

Live a long life!

In recent years, two of your dear friends got married. I attended both weddings. Shivani got married into a wonderful joint family. Her husband lives with his family consisting of his parents, two sisters, two elder brothers and their wives along with five kids between them. Shivani's mother had been worried. Before the match was fixed, she had said to me, "What should I do? We really like the boy, but Shivani will have to live in a joint family. A family of fifteen people! I don't know how she will get along with everyone."

I reminded her, "Your family also has ten people. Three generations live together—your mother-in-law as well as your daughter-in-law. And Shivani is very attached to both her grandmother and her sister-in-law. She is dear to all because she is the only daughter. If she gets along well with everyone in your house, why would she not at her in-laws'?"

Shivani's mother had not considered the situation in her own home. The reality is that a daughter remains a child to us until she gets married. As if she was born yesterday. While we raise daughters, we keep thinking, "She has to go to a different house one day. We don't expect her to do much housework." If she makes a mistake, we tell her, "This will not do in your in-laws' house."

What we do not realize is that daughters keep preparing

themselves mentally to go to their in-laws' house. They learn how to behave in a relationship from their mothers, their sisters-in-law, and other family and relatives. Indirectly, they ingrain the qualities and *sanskaars* (values) for becoming a daughter-in-law. They learn to adapt themselves to different relationships. After the wedding, they assume the role of not only a wife, but also a daughter-in-law, a sister-in-law, an aunt, and many others.

Every relationship has its special warmth. Each one has different emotions and comes with its own set of expectations. A girl suddenly assumes so many titles after getting married. She is only a little prepared for them, but with time, she learns to adapt herself to each relationship. Sometimes I wonder at women's educational, professional, and familial roles. Education and work are required to make life happy and smooth; there is training provided for those. However, the art of maintaining relationships is also very important for a happy and smooth life. Even an unmarried person has relationships to maintain, even though these are fewer than a married person's. There is no education or training provided for this aspect of life. Despite that, our girls can successfully manage their relationships. The main reason for this is the informal training they receive while they are growing up in their families. Therefore, in our society we consider it important to match the *sanskaars* of the two families at the time of marriage. I met Shivani a few days ago. Her face was showing how happy she is in her in-laws' house full of people.

Your other friend Shalini is married into a family where it's just her husband. No other family member lives with them. Shalini is happy with her husband, but there is certainly a sense of inadequacy. She feels lonely. She said to me, "Aunty, I quite like living just with my husband. But when I return exhausted from work, I wish someone was there to make a cup of tea for me. Or even to ask how my day went."

Before the wedding, Shalini lived with her parents, siblings, and her grandmother. It had been her decision to marry Rahul and she is happy. But she wishes to share her happiness.

In their different circumstances, Shivani and Shalini have their respective comforts and problems. It is true that humans crave what they do not have. But it is also true that nature has made a woman to be a giver. That's why she was given a womb in her body, and breasts to carry milk. As she gives birth to a child, gives her milk to the child, a woman gets used to giving. The framework of family and social life has been structured in such a way that women came to have the role of a giver. This is how the giving *sanskaar* of a woman keeps getting handed down the generations.

Social life is going through a transition these days. People want to adopt new ways of life, leaving old values behind. For example, newly-weds want to live by themselves away from their families. This is a new trend. However, people have not yet forgotten the comforts and joys of a joint family. That's why some people also long for the presence of elderly relatives in their house.

I wanted you to know that Shivani and Shalini are both living their various relationships wonderfully after getting married. Her parents' darling Shivani is giving a lot of love and care to her brother-in-law and sister-in-law and that makes me very happy. Shivani's mother was not so sure. But daughters have some very special qualities. When the time comes, those qualities manifest themselves. I am reminded of an incident from forty years ago. A friend of mine was very worried. I asked, "What happened?"

"My in-laws are coming from the village tomorrow," she said.

"So what?" I asked.

"What do you mean 'so what?' You have gotten used to living with your in-laws. I live alone with my husband. I am very scared of them."

Her days with her in-laws kept passing and so did her anxiety. By now she has gotten two daughters married. I met her recently. She said, "I got my daughters married into families where the groom's parents live in the same house. They will have comfortable lives."

Your brother Nawin got married fifteen years ago. In the initial days after their wedding, I used to cook something new for your sister-in-law Sangita every day. When Nawin visited his in-laws', Sangita's grandmother asked, "How does my granddaughter get along in the house?" It is natural for a girl's family to be concerned for her after the wedding. Nawin joked, "Your granddaughter is a couch potato. My mother cooks and feeds her. She eats the food and says, 'that was delicious!'"

Sangita's grandmother was relieved and happy, "That's why it helps to have a young mother-in-law. The girl can live comfortably in the in-laws' house for some time."

The belief system of our rural life was so clear. Five years ago, I went to America. Praveen's wife Kalpana was pregnant, and I wanted to go stay with them for some time. I was very busy with work in India at that time, but one must fulfil their family responsibilities. Praveen and Kalpana had not expected me to go and stay with them for a month. I could not think of not staying close to Kalpana at a time like that. As soon as I reached, I started cooking. I used to ask Kalpana after every meal, "Did you like it?"

"That was delicious!" she used to say. I used to feel so satisfied.

I later found out that some of Kalpana's friends had warned her when she had told them that I was going to visit. "It's not easy living with your mother-in-law," they had said. One of her friends in America told her that when her first son was born, her Indian in-laws had started keeping the child primarily with them. She had not liked this intrusion of privacy. When her second child was born, she used to lock herself in her room with the child to prevent her in-laws from taking control of him as well. Kalpana told me she did not find it too burdensome to live with me for a month. It is expected that there would be some issues. However, if people are determined to adjust and make it work, it does work out.

It is pleasurable to live together with family. You become knowledgeable in social and family life without reading books. The knowledge and experiences keep getting passed down the generations smoothly. These days, new circumstances are giving rise to nuclear families. It is not very easy to return to the joint family system. But we should try to maintain our relationships to whatever extent possible.

Girls have the special ability to handle all kinds of situations. That is why daughters are special.

Your Mom

□

Equality of Bride and Groom

Dear Mili,

May you always be happy!

It is the season of weddings. A wedding conducted according to Hindu tradition involves finding an auspicious date for the wedding. On the day of the wedding, the auspicious time is decided. Recently, I spoke with several families that are searching for grooms for their daughters. Yesterday, Mr. Mohan Mishra visited. He said, "We have found a suitable match for our daughter. He comes from a good family. Their *sanskaars* match ours. The boy is good-looking, and his temperament matches well with our daughter's."

"Then what's the wait? You can fix the wedding date," I said.

"We are thinking. They are a good match in terms of their education and qualifications. However, our daughter has better test scores than the boy at all levels."

I said, "What all factors are you going to try to match? Religion, sect, temperament, and other qualities—all these match. Now if the girl has better test scores than the boy, does it really matter?"

"Yes, it does matter. We have always believed that the boy should be somewhat superior to the girl, if not her equal."

I started thinking how we are still not able to break free of our traditional thinking.

Society expects the groom to be superior to the bride.

In our history, girls used to choose a suitable match for themselves by way of a *svayamvar*. And they chose to marry men who are superior to them in every way—looks, intelligence, fame, abilities, and income. As time passed, girls were deprived of the right to choose their own grooms. Their parents took on the responsibility to find their life partners. The girls were not even consulted. However, the basis of the parents' groom search process too used to be that the groom should be superior to the bride. The mindset was developed over the years as people heard or read stories from our history of *svayamvars* where girls chose their own husbands.

The story of Vidyottama and Kalidas is a popular one. This is how the story goes. Vidyottama was a highly educated girl. Her father grew concerned when she became of marriageable age. He was aware of his daughter's intellect and qualities. It was not easy to find a suitable match for her. A *svayamvar* had to be conducted. Many highly educated men started lining up. Vidyottama used to hold debates with them on the interpretation of the Shastras (Hindu scriptures). The men would get defeated and return home disappointed after losing hopes of marrying a famous woman like Vidyottama. Word spread far and wide about Vidyottama's prowess. Fathers of young men who were defeated in debates by Vidyottama were displeased.

Scholars and intellectuals were also discussing this situation. Some people started getting jealous of Vidyottama's intellectual prowess. They decided to teach her a lesson. They came up with a plan to find an uneducated, dimwitted man. They set off in their search. One young man was sitting on a tree branch and sawing it, but he was sitting on the part of the branch which was going to fall. When they saw this scene, they realized that there could be no one else in the world more stupid than him. They talked to him and made him agree to marry Vidyottama.

They trained him and told him, "You will have to talk to Vidyottama only in gestures. Whatever she asks, respond only with your hand and facial gestures."

Vidyottama's father was growing more concerned about her wedding. These people went and said to him, "We have found a very handsome and intelligent young man for your daughter. If you allow, we can have him converse with your daughter."

Vidyottama's father replied, "Only conversing with my daughter is not enough. He will have to engage in an intellectual debate with her."

"Yes, yes," they said, "he will engage in a debate. At a very young age, he is already at the pinnacle of knowledge and intellect."

"Sure, if you say so. Please ask him to come."

A date was fixed. Vidyottama's father was pleased with the handsome looks of the young man. Arrangements were made for a debate to be held in the courtyard. When Vidyottama was seated, one scholar said, "He is observing silence today. He will answer your questions, but only in gestures. He cannot break his vow of silence."

Vidyottama was annoyed, but she agreed to the condition. The young man had a bright face. Vidyottama felt that she could trust the scholars. She started the intellectual debate in gestures. Vidyottama raised one finger towards the sky. In response, the young man raised two fingers towards the sky. The scholars in the audience applauded. Next, Vidyottama raised all five fingers. The young man responded by showing his fist. The scholars applauded again. It was concluded that the young man's intellectual prowess was no less than that of Vidyottama. In fact, he seemed more knowledgeable than her. In his answers, he had combined philosophy with practicality. Vidyottama had raised one finger to show that there is only one God. The scholars interpreted that the young man's response with two fingers showed that he believed in Dualism, a school of thought that suggests that God and human souls are distinct entities. When Vidyottama raised five fingers, they were meant to depict the five senses. The young man had raised his fist in response and the scholars interpreted, "He is saying that one should keep their five senses in control."

Everyone burst in joy. Vidyottama and the young man got married. On the wedding night, Vidyottama started a conversation with him in Sanskrit. She heard a camel bleating outside and asked, "what animal is that?" Her husband said, "it is a camel." Because of his pronunciation of words, she began to doubt that he was a scholar. She asked him more questions. Her husband admitted that he was illiterate. He was just a woodworker. He was forced to marry her by the scholars. He told her the whole scheme the scholars had come up with. Vidyottama was heartbroken, but now it was too late—she was married to this man.

She thought for some time and then said to him, "You should leave. Make yourself worthy of speaking to me, then come back."

Vidyottama's husband had become entranced by her beauty and her patience. He was also in awe of her intelligence. He left but was determined to win her back. He started praying to Goddess Kali. The Goddess was pleased with his devotion. He asked the Goddess to grant his wish of becoming a scholar. The Goddess said, "You will gain the knowledge of every book you touch tonight." He spent the entire night touching every book of scriptures that was stored in the temple. The knowledge of the scriptures got transferred to him and by the next morning he was a serious scholar. When he returned to Vidyottama, she tested him again. She was very pleased with his knowledge and admired her luck for being his wife. The young man continued his education and came to be known as Kalidas. Kalidas has written several important books, including the epics Meghdoot and Kumar Sambhav. Kalidas is considered one of the greatest writers of ancient India. His literature is very inspiring for writers and poets.

The story of Kalidas's wedding and his way of becoming a scholar has become an idiom in our lives. When a child says, "I have read everything. I have it all memorized," his parents will remark, "Oh, so you have become Kalidas!"

One thing this story shows is that girls are not happy marrying someone who is lesser than them in age or ability. It is notable that several world-famous scholars were younger than their wives. However, the truth is that even today, girls prefer to marry men who are superior to them—in age, intellect, strength, and wealth. However, this story also shows that Kalidas became Kalidas because of his wife. In our village there are several men who were taught how to read and write by their wives. There are also many examples from the villages of the wives who sold their property or jewelry to finance their husbands' education.

In fact, a wife considers her husband's wealth, strength, and knowledge to be her own. She takes pride in her husband's pride. That's why she invests herself in making her husband successful.

My mother was not very educated, but she was very proud because her husband was one of the few educated people in the village. She cared for him a lot. She believed her husband was special and considered herself special by virtue of being married to an educated man. The uneducated wife of a schoolteacher (Master) was also addressed as a teacher (*Masterni*)—this was a big deal for her.

Today, girls choose their life partners from amongst their fellow students. This is a good thing. They get to spend time with their friends and get to know them. However, the incidence of divorce is also greater in these marriages. In many of these marriages, a battle of superiority starts soon after and when both are equal in age and ability, who will listen to the other? The belief system for matchmaking in our society has been developed after much thought and consideration. There is no harm in following it. Not all old beliefs are wrong, and not every new belief should be accepted without evaluating it. It is important to find a middle path.

With love,
Mom

□

After Marrying a Daughter Off

Dear Mili,

Tons of Blessings!

These days in India some places are experiencing extreme winter, while other places are warm, and yet others are hot. One of the special qualities of our land is that at any given time, there is an opportunity to enjoy all kinds of weather. Along with this warm-cold season is also widespread the season of weddings. I attend many weddings and give my blessings to the couples. Every year thousands of girls and boys tie the knot. I miss you a lot. The time has come for you to get married. According to our Shastras (scriptures), it is the duty of parents to make sure their children are married at the appropriate age. The scriptures advise that the age of twenty-five or above is suitable for marriage. Until twenty-five years is the phase of *bramhacharya* during which a person gains education. It is only after one is skilled to earn a living that they should start a family—this is what our scriptures advise. During an episode in our history, due to some reason, girls and boys started getting married at a very young age. Generations went by following this tradition. Our social thinkers turned their attention towards this problem and the movement to end child-marriage gained momentum.

Indian society is full of contradictions. Even today, young children are getting married off in some parts of the country, while in other places there are men and women in their thirties who are unmarried. Some people get so busy in making their careers that they forget to get married. It is the parents' duty to remind their children when it is the right time to get married. Children are now taking on this responsibility as their own. This type of a wedding is not new for our society. In fact, our Shastras have allowed for eight kinds of weddings and *gandharva vivah* (love marriage where a bride and groom choose each other) is one of them. This is a land of diversity and variety.

I have come to appreciate the significance of marriage even more through the emotions conveyed by the wedding folksongs from Mithilanchal (region where people speak Mithila, encompassing parts of the states of Bihar and Jharkhand, and Terai of Nepal). I have also taught those folksongs to you. I remember you singing those songs in your sweet voice while also internalizing the emotion conveyed by them.

These folksongs are also known as *sanskaar geet* (songs that teach traditions and values). The guidelines conveyed by these songs apply not only to the bride and groom, but also to the entire society. It is not that marriages did not dissolve in our society. In all stages and sections of our society, marriages have broken. However, the ideal of a wedding dictates the relationship between a husband and wife is for life. This is true not just in India—all over the world, stability is considered central to an ideal marriage.

A debate has begun in the world on how the relationship between a man and woman, especially a husband and a wife, should be. Various definitions are provided for a life partner. When I think of this issue in an Indian context, I am surprised. Sita's mother-in-law Kaushalya (in the ancient epic Ramayana) had blessed her, "May your marriage be eternal—like the waters in Ganga and Yamuna rivers."

You had this verse from Ramcharitmanas (epic poem written by Tulsidas in the sixteenth century on the story of Rama) memorized since childhood. I used to write this verse on the cash envelopes I gifted to the newlywed girls. Ever since you learnt how to write, you took on the task of writing the verse on the envelopes. You were already writing and reading "Delhi is the capital of India" in Hindi since you were four years old. You used to read verses from Ramcharitmanas without any help. Sometimes I feel I was not fair to you. In those days I was writing my novel, "Nayi Devyani." You wanted to be close to me and would not stop talking and asking questions. I decided to get you a slate chalkboard so that you would stay occupied. You started learning the Hindi alphabet on that chalkboard. By the end of the two months it took me to complete the novel, you had learnt how to read and write complex Hindi words and sentences. People used to be amazed by your Hindi.

I digress so much when I start remembering your childhood. So, I was saying that the blessing given to the newlywed Sita by her mother-in-law Kaushalya has a special meaning. The blessing benefits Rama. Only if Rama lives a long life, Sita's marriage can last as long as the waters in Ganga and Yamuna rivers. This is the ultimate goal for an ideal marriage. It is like the relationship between words and meaning, flowers and scent, voice and sweetness, and the Ardhanarishwara (half-man, half-woman) image of God Shiva and Goddess Parvati. It is impossible to imagine one person's existence without the other. Man and woman are a supreme example of equality and they represent the concept of Ardhanarishwara.

The Western and Eastern perspectives on marriages are so different. This Indian perspective on marriage is ancient as well as modern. The Western world is tired of the marriages breaking and its negative impact on the children involved. They are looking for ways to prevent marriages from breaking.

I had the opportunity to meet several couples in America. I analyzed their daily behavior. The husband and wife spend very little time living for each-other, in other words, they have very little time to depend on each-other. They have their own car, own office, own bank account, their own dreams for life. Then where is the marriage? Where is the couple? They will have different joys and sorrows. Losses and benefits are personal too.

Your *Nani* (maternal grandmother) was called *Masterniji* (female teacher) in our village. She was illiterate; never went to school. But everyone in the village called her *Masterniji*. Only because her husband was a Master (schoolteacher). She would be overjoyed when the village people addressed her as *Masterniji*. She was very proud of her husband being a schoolmaster. However, her daughter (your mother) did not like to be called *Professorani* (female professor) or *Mantrani* (female Minister). I am me; he is him. In just one generation, things changed. Now, whether that *Masterniji* lived a happier life or I—that's a matter of further research.

When I think of your wedding, another incident from your childhood comes to mind. You started accompanying me to Mahila Dakhshata Samiti (women's welfare committee) meetings from a very young age (four years). You would sit in my lap and listen to the discussions. Those days dowry-related women issues were on the rise. One day I overheard you and your brother Parimal talking. Someone in our neighborhood had passed away. You two started discussing the associated social and family problems. Your brother said, "Everyone dies when they get old."

"Our mom and dad will die too?" you had asked.

"Yes," Parimal said.

"Oh, no! Then who will give dowry for my wedding?"

All of us seated in the adjacent room listening to your concerns about your future could not stop laughing. Your father asked, "How much dowry will you take?" You counted the fingers on one hand one-by-one and said, "Five hundred Rupees?"

"Only five-hundred! Then I will find a groom for you today!" your father said.

We have not been able to find a groom for you until now; nor have you. We have decided, however, to not give dowry. We have given you education and knowledge, and don't feel the need to gather any gifts for your dowry. In fact, gifts given with love and within the parents' financial means do not fall under the category of dangerous dowry—the kind that is infecting the boys' parents these days and scaring the girls' parents. It has been common for a girl's father to start gathering gifts for a daughter from the time she is born, gift those to her at the time of the wedding and feel relieved after giving away his daughter's hand in marriage (kanyadaan). Groom's family has continued to be chosen by matching the qualities with those of the bride's family. Indian folksongs convey this emotion too—a father can sleep without any worries after marrying his daughter into a good family.

Things are completely different now. Parents do not feel relieved after sending their daughter to the in-law's house. They keep wondering if someone is going to start complaining from her in-law's side. How much they are going to continue asking in dowry—these thoughts keep them up at night. This is why many people now consider a daughter to be a burden.

Nowadays girls and boys have started fearing the beautiful concept of marriage. I hope you have no such fear. So far you have only been focused on your career—that is a good thing. Now start thinking about marriage. I am trying to find a family whose qualities match ours and a groom compatible with you. You should look as well. Let's see who finds him first. In any case, start developing a positive attitude towards marriage. Leading a married life is also a duty. Do not marry for entertainment, marry to fulfil your familial duties. I started looking for a prospective groom today.

Rest later...
Your Mom

□

Nal-Damyanti

Beloved daughter Mili,

Best Wishes!

You loved listening to stories in your childhood. You made us tell you stories and asked so many questions about them. It was difficult to answer some of your questions given how young you were. The stories and folktales from our ancient history have their own messages and goals. The meaning of the stories you listen to as a child is often understood when you grow up. I too used to listen to stories and tales from the Ramayana and the Mahabharata and other folk tales from my grandmothers. I did not understand the significance of those stories as a child. Now when I think about the characters from those old stories, I realize that those characters' life stories are very useful for us even today.

Usually, stories and their ideals are relevant to the period they are written in, however, there are certain characters in our ancient scriptures whose stories will continue to inspire in all time periods. There is no shortage of women in these characters. These women were no less in intellectual and physical strength as compared to men; sometimes even superior.

Damyanti is one such woman. These eternal women in our history have come to be known as Sati. Sati is a woman who walks on the path of truth (Sat). Sati Damyanti's character is an inspiration for women—of this generation as well as of future generations. I feel sad that the young girls in our society are not made aware of these women characters from our history—neither at home nor at school. Parents do not tell these stories to children, nor are the stories included in the schools' curriculum.

Damyanti's story goes like this. King Bheeshma was the ruler of Vidharva. The king had four children—three sons and one daughter. The daughter's name was Damyanti. She was not only beautiful, but also very intelligent and clever. In no time, Damyanti became a young woman. Those days in the kingdom of Nishadh, Veersen's son Nal reigned on the throne. Nal was also a multitalented person. It was common for people to travel between Vidharva and Nishadh. People from each kingdom used to sing praises of their King Nal and Princess Damyanti in the other kingdom. Nal and Damyanti had heard about each other's qualities as well and were attracted to each other without ever meeting.

The story also describes that Nal and Damyanti used to communicate with each other via a swan. The swan used to carry their love notes along with the emotion of love. The Gods also came to know of the qualities of Nal and Damyanti, as well as of their relationship. In Damyanti's *svayamvar* (groom-selection ceremony), the Gods appeared in the disguise of Nal. However, Damyanti recognized the real Nal and put the wedding garland around his neck. They started living happily. They had a son and a daughter. Nal had many talents, but he had one fault—he was addicted to gambling. Then one day, he lost all his wealth in a gamble. They went to live in a forest and suffered many pains.

One day, Nal and Damyanti were sleeping, covered in the only piece of clothing they had between them. Nal cut the sheet of cloth in half, covered Damyanti's body with one half of the cloth, tied the other half around his waist and left quietly while she was sleeping. When Damyanti woke up, she started looking for her husband desperately. She roamed across the forests searching for him and reached the kingdom of the learned King Sahau. The queen listened to her story in detail and invited her to stay with them. Damyanti posed some conditions for agreeing to stay with them. The queen accepted all her conditions and called her daughter Sunanda and told her, "This woman is going through a hardship. But she is a king's daughter and a king's wife. So, you should treat her as a friend."

Elsewhere, Nal met a snake while wandering around. The snake became his friend. The snake gave him two special pieces of clothing. On his request, Nal changed his name to Bahuk. Here, Damyanti managed to reach her father's house and told her tragic story to her mother. The king sent out messengers in search of his son-in-law Nal. One messenger came back to report that Bahuk (Nal) was taking care of horses in the stables of the king of Ayodhya. The king said, "Damyanti's husband Nal left her sleeping in the forest. Now her second *svayamvar* is being planned. I need to go see Nal as soon as possible."

Nal was very upset after hearing about the *svayamvar*. But he was the king's servant now. Damyanti sent her maid to keep an eye on Nal's activities. The maid came back and reported on many special qualities of his personality. Damyanti was convinced that Bahuk was in fact her husband Nal in a different getup. Then she sent both her kids to him. Bahuk started crying on seeing his children.

The maid came back to the palace and gave this news to Damyanti. She grew more confident in her belief that Bahuk was indeed Nal, and with her mother's permission, she asked for Bahuk to be brought in her palace. When he faced her, she said, "One pious man deceived his wife by leaving her asleep in the forest. That man is Nal and I am his wife Damyanti. You haven't seen Nal, have you?" Nal burst out, "No, no. I did not deceive you and my kingdom on purpose. This is fate's doing." They both burst into tears. Nal was curious as to why Damyanti had planned another *svayamvar*. She said, "That announcement was just a ploy to make you come here. There is no other horse rider like you on this earth who could reach here in such a short time."

The two started living happily. This story of Nal-Damyanti highlights many things. Damyanti certainly had an intelligent mind, patience, and a keen eye. She had decided to marry Nal. Therefore, in her *svayamvar*, she rejected the Gods disguised as Nal and chose to marry Nal. Many Gods were present there in the form of Nal. However, Damyanti had the power to distinguish between the behavior of Gods and those of humans, and using that power, she chose Nal amongst the Gods and placed the garland around his neck.

Her decision shows that she recognized the qualities of Nal and did not care about leading a life of comfort. She did not lose her self-respect even during hardship. After getting separated from her husband, in a state of despair and suffering, she reached a king. The queen was ready to give her shelter, but Damyanti posed some conditions for her stay. It was unusual for a person seeking shelter to come up with conditions. The scheme to draw Nal back to herself by pretending to hold a second *svayamvar* also shows Damyanti's devotion and clever intelligence. Nal's personality also had special features.

In today's world, our daughters should have some women role models to look up to. Families are breaking apart at a fast pace. Husband and wife no longer have unfailing trust in each other. The effect of families breaking because of small reasons is seen on the next generation and the elderly in the family. In times like these, it is important to present a character such as that of Damyanti as an ideal for the youth.

Share this story with the girls studying with you. Even the boys—because at the time of choosing a girl to be their friend or a life partner, not only is their educational qualification important, but so is their character. Boys should also know and understand these things. These characteristic qualities in boys and girls (young men and women are also called boys and girls) bring harmony and consistency to life, as well as joy. If husband and wife have complete trust in each other, then even dark days of life can become brighter.

Your Mom ☐

Pre-Marital Counseling

Daughter Mili,

Always stay happy!

I am reminiscing your childhood again today. You were always glued to me. On seeing this, your Ashwini Uncle used to remark that we were like a braid and hair tie—inseparable. All daughters are like that with their mothers. However, the daughters are destined to get separated from their mothers and settle down somewhere far away. That is why a thinker has compared a daughter's life to that of a paddy plant. The seeds of paddy are sown in one field and once the samplings grow, they are transplanted to another field. But when they are transplanted, the saplings become yellow for a few days. After some time, the samplings acclimatize to the new conditions and start flourishing. A daughter faces a similar situation. It does take some time for a daughter to get used to playing the role of a daughter-in-law.

During this time, a girl needs the support of her in-laws. In-laws are expected to shower their affection on the newlywed girl and help her get accustomed to her new home. Similarly, the girls are expected to exercise patience in getting acclimatized to and transplanted in the new conditions, to take time to understand everyone in the in-laws' house.

Last week, a newly married young lady, Anubha, visited. She said to me, "Aunty, please help us get a divorce. I can't stand to live even another minute with that man!"

She had come to the "Family Counseling Center" with her complaint. I asked, "How long have you been married?"

She said, "Aunty, it has been three months. I have understood this man very well. Now I cannot live with him. Please help me get a divorce fast, aunty."

It was apparent from her demeanor that she was really in a hurry. I was certain that she had made the decision to get married in a hurry too. Now she was in a hurry to get rid of her husband. But it got me thinking. She understood her husband in just three months. She must be a Goddess in human form because it can take not just one, but seven lives, and still a married couple may never completely understand each other. Everyone finds their partner wonderful at times, and terrible at other times. A different person can never be completely what our mind desires That is why, for one reason or another, a married life is mostly about making adjustments.

Marriage is not for entertainment, nor is it only to fulfil our wishes. It is a duty—to live together for personal needs and to grow a family. We have been explaining the significance of marriage to the young boys and girls in our family and friend circles. Children ingrain the *sanskaars* (values) by watching their parents. Our folksongs have also been teaching the importance of marriage, the responsibilities of husbands and wives, and the tips and tricks to sustain the sweetness of the relationship. For the last three decades, social institutions have been operating "Family Counseling Centers." Men or women who are victims of marital abuse have been bringing their complaints to these centers. They are given appropriate advice. These centers try their best to prevent the marriages from breaking. However, there have also been cases where marriages have been broken by giving legal advice in situations where a couple could have lived compatibly with each other. In the last ten years, Family Counseling Centers across the nation have received more than 30 lakh (3 million) cases.

After seeing Anubha's case, I realized that now our society also needs "Pre-marital Counseling Centers." The work that used to be done by family and society by way of festivals and rituals, folksongs, and traditions, will now have to be done by social organizations. The society of yesterday was different from the society today. Today's problems are new and different—as the problems change form with time, so do the people involved in solving those problems. These organizations are also now responsible for giving information to the youth about the various aspects of marriage.

The truth is that marriage is not a requirement for anyone, nor should it be. But there should be a requirement to sustain a marriage because when a marriage breaks it affects not just the couple, but also the children as well as the elderly in the household. This does not mean that people should continue to suffer in abusive marriages and not complain. In those situations, it is better to get separated and live happily. But a deep and meaningful relationship such as marriage should not get broken due to minor issues.

People in the Western world are often surprised by the marital arrangements and conditions in India. It is a result of our deep and multi-faceted culture and tradition. Lord Shiva and Goddess Parvati are the best example amongst the Gods for an ideal married life. According to the scriptures, it was Parvati who chose Shiva to be her life partner, not Shiva. She had taken a vow to marry Shiva or to stay unmarried her entire life.

A marriage creates family life, a household. Parvati had to run that household, that's why she prays to the Gods and chooses a suitable husband for herself. But who was her chosen husband? He was a vagabond saint, with no house or land of his own. No wealth, no possessions. Parvati knew all this and still chose Shiva to be her husband. Folktales and folksongs provide a unique description of Shiva and Parvati's married life. The characters of these Gods and Goddesses as well as those of women from our ancient storybooks are reflected in bits and pieces even in today's women. From childhood, the seeds of these qualities are sown in them by way of the folktales and folksongs.

Listening to Anubha and seeing her eagerness to get a divorce, I was reminded of your Savitri *mami* (maternal aunt). You may be surprised by her name—who is Savitri *mami*? She is your Kameshwar *mama*'s (maternal uncle) wife. You must be smiling now thinking of her. She is that kind of person. Three months ago, we had gone to the village to attend your cousin Julie's (Savitri's niece) wedding. Kameshwar *mama* was performing the rituals for giving the bride's hand in marriage (*kanyadaan*). Your Savitri *mami* was seated next to him in the *mandap* (marriage pavilion). Your heavy-bodied Kameshwar *mama* had to remain seated on the floor for two hours to perform the rituals. Then the priest said, "Now you may leave."

Kameshwar *mama* raised his arm towards his wife standing close by. Your slim and frail *mami* used all her strength to lift your *mama* up from his seated position. The entire courtyard was filled with people—their two grown-up sons, cousins, and extended family. After all, by applying all his strength and with his wife's support, Kameshwar *mama* was able to rise to his feet. But I became tearful, and they were tears of happiness. Your Sangita *bhabhi* (sister-in-law) was seated next to me and she asked, "what's the matter?"

I said, "Didn't you see? The woman who just supported him in standing up could have left him forty years ago for his behavior in their married life. Their marriage was full of ups and downs. She did not leave him. Not only that, but she also pulled him back from many wrong directions he walked in. She made him a good family man. Now at this age these two are very affectionate towards each other. The credit for this goes to Savitri *bhabhi*, to her patience and her farsightedness."

So, I was telling you about "Pre-marital Counseling Centers." We have started our institution on behalf of the Central Social Welfare Board. We have launched thirty-five workshops across the country. In a workshop organized by a Delhi institution, Sampoorna, a woman psychologist who has been living in London for the last twenty-five years participated. She was pleased to see these workshops. She said, "You have taken the lead in these matters over the Western countries. They are suffering badly because of marital problems in their societies. No one has even thought of pre-marital counseling in those countries."

I said, "We will teach them how to solve those problems. This type of counseling is part of our tradition. Now as the social fabric is changing, the form of counseling is also evolving." This has also become important as people get so focused on their careers that they do not even think of marriage until they are in their thirties. They feel nervous thinking of marriage.

I once asked a 35-year-old woman, "when do you plan to get married?"

She said, "I haven't thought about it."

"Then you shouldn't think about getting married," I said.

Our ancestors, while imaging a lifespan of a hundred years for every individual, suggested four stages (*ashrams*) of life: *bramhacharya* (the student life), *grihasth* (the married life), *vaanprasth* (the retired life), and *sanyaas* (the life of renunciation). Each phase consists of twenty-five years. If you study this concept closely, you will be surprised to learn that this division of life is compatible with a man or woman's physical, mental, and emotional needs. *Grihasth ashram* (the married life), on which the other three phases are based, has been given the most prominence.

You are living far away from your own soil but do try to read and understand the social history of India. It is not just history. It is also our present, and it will also be our future. Make your friends from other countries aware of these points from our history. I believe that by adopting a few of our Indian social and family values, the Western world can solve some of its problems. This does not mean that we should not learn from them. This is an exchange of *sanskritis* (cultural wisdom). Each side has some positives. We should learn from them too.

More in next month's letter.
Your Mom

□

Compassion: A Heart's Decoration

Dear daughter Mili,

Blessings!

These days I reminisce about your childhood a lot. I do not know if you remember these incidents as well. You were very young. Probably eight or nine years old. We had planned to organize a social event called "*Holi-Milan*" (a get-together to celebrate the festival of colors, Holi). At that time, you got Chicken Pox. I was having a hard time coming to terms with celebrating a festival while a child was sick at home. My heart was not into planning the event.

Your Ashwini Uncle (Member of Parliament) and I were talking over breakfast one morning. He asked, "How is the preparation for *Holi-Milan* coming along?"

I replied, "It's coming along at a slow pace. Some people are working on it. But I am not able to devote complete attention to it because Mili is sick."

You were in bed and intently following our conversation. You exclaimed, "Why? Why are you people worried about me? You live your own lives, let me be."

We were both stunned by the grave life thought coming out of your young mouth. An eight-year-old girl was talking about "living your own lives." We were unable to speak for a few minutes. Then Ashwiniji said, "Really? We should live our own lives and not think about you? Why? You are a part of each of our lives. You are our life. Then how can we not think about you?"

His tone was reprimanding, like that of an older Uncle. You used to be a little scared of him. He used to find it sad that you would not talk freely with him. In that moment, you did not give him a response. Actually, the words spoken around you made an impression on your mind and you blurted them out without thought. You were too young to ponder over and analyze those life values. But you had started internalizing words, sentences, and emotions from your surroundings. Your Ashwini *chacha* (paternal uncle) had said something deep. At that time, you could not understand their meaning. When I think of your life and behavior so far, I feel that in your "own life" you have absorbed many other lives. Even in your current student life, your life is not just yours.

When I think about incidents from your childhood, I feel you were so full of compassion. You thought about everyone and did whatever little you could within your ability to help them. Even in your childhood, your life was not just "your own."

There is an incident I can never forget. Nor can your cousin, Raju. Your *phua* (paternal aunt) Prabha Benipuri's son Raju was studying at Delhi University in those days. He is around eighteen years older than you. You were around three-four years old. He got infected with Chicken Pox. We brought him home from his dorm. You were instructed to not go close to him. Even at that small age you would follow instructions given by elders—that was a special quality of yours. You would not go close to him. You would sit outside his bedroom door—sometimes on a chair or just on the floor—and narrate endless stories and incidents to your cousin. You were not enrolled in a school yet. That's why most of the stories were either made-up by you or the ones we had told you. Sometimes you would talk, and sometimes you would even dance for him. You would entertain him for hours and help him pass time. He developed a special affection for you in his heart—and it is still alive.

You would take care of your disabled brother Parimal, help him move and lie down. Your little hands were forever in his service. You would open his books for him, help him move his limbs, help him lie down on bed. At times, his head would slip out of your small hands and hit the corner of a bed frame or a chair. Even if he was hurt, he would never complain and would never want you to leave his company. You, too, used to enjoy his company a lot.

I used to tell you a story every day. Dhruv, Aaruni, Eklavya, Prahlaad, Nachiketa—you would listen to the childhood stories of these characters from Hindu scriptures with all your heart. Your facial expressions would change as you heard the stories. You used to love the stories of Luv-Kush (twin boys of Lord Rama and his wife Sita). You also liked the story of Dhruv. I used to ask you to re-tell the stories after you had heard them a few times. But one day when I asked you to re-tell the story of Shravan Kumar, you teared up. You said, "Mom, I won't tell you that story. It hurts my heart. Mom, can you make Shravan Kumar's parents alive in the story?" Now when I think back about those incidents, I feel your childhood was different from others'. Your feelings and emotions have expanded as you have grown. That's why you stand out amongst friends of your age. Many of your elder cousins often say, "Mili is special, different from everyone." This gives strength to my belief that if a person has a special quality, it cannot be kept hidden. Most people will recognize it. The compassionate heart of that person touches even those who lack compassion in their hearts. Even after having sent you across the seven seas, I am assured that you must be making bonds with friends and teachers around you because of these special qualities you have. This bonding is what makes a human being human.

Our cook Rekha was bonded with you with all her heart. She got infected by tuberculosis and was admitted in a hospital for six months. In a similar situation, any household with children would not have accepted Rekha back in the household. I had doubts too. Seeing me lost in thought, you said, "Mom, if I had this disease, would you not have brought me back home?" I got her home the very next day. You would make her sleep in your room, teach her, and inquire about her nutrition. She graduated from high school. As your departure for America grew closer, we were all sad. But the saddest person in the house was Rekha.

After a few months, it was your niece Hansa's birthday. Many people were over for dinner at our house that evening. Everyone left by ten pm. We were all seated in the living room when we heard Rekha crying loudly in the kitchen. When we inquired, she said, "Last year Mili *didi* (elder sister) was here. There was a big pile of dishes after the party. She had sent me out of the kitchen and had done all the dishes for me." In that moment we found Rekha's words amusing. Later I realized that things that did not occur to us came naturally to you.

Humans bond with each other by way of these small things. This type of behavior makes life happier for a person. I sometimes feel that a person who lives solely for oneself cannot find joy in life. Those who live for others, even in small ways, find many joyful moments in life.

Please keep your special qualities alive. Never let the flow of compassion dry out. After all, even across the seven seas, you live with humans. So what if the country is different or the attire is different? Where there are humans there will be compassion. Compassion helps human beings bond with each other and that bonding keeps bringing joy.

I hope your compassion will stay alive and thriving.
Your Mom

□

The Importance of *Saghor*

Dear Mili,

Blessings!

The other day, I felt great satisfaction after hearing the news from you. I realized that we should keep teaching our children about the traditions and rituals of our society. We should also continually tell them about the familial or societal relevance underlying those traditions. Children continue the traditions when they grow up. When your two elder brothers were very young, your father used to say, "My life is like an open book for them. Children don't need to be lectured. Whatever we want to teach, is how we should behave ourselves. Children learn more by watching than by listening."

Sometimes I used to be annoyed at such talk. But I have now come to the conclusion that he was absolutely right. Your sister-in-law Sangita often says about her husband Nawin, "He talks and behaves exactly like his father."

When you told me over the phone that even in America you invited your friend for *Mehmani* (a special dinner party for the bride-to-be) before she left for India for her wedding—I was thrilled. You told me, "Some of my other girlfriends came too. They asked me what *Mehmani* means. I told them what you had told me—that a bride-to-be is invited for dinner to each of her relatives' homes before the wedding. That custom is called *Mehmani* (in the state of Bihar)." You also told me how all your friends started discussing the emotions and significance behind the various Indian customs and rituals and someone commented how great India is. Indian girls came to learn about Indian customs in America.

Two days ago, I was in Rajasthan's Doongarpur district. Women from many villages had come to participate in the meeting. When I mentioned in my speech the incidence of you treating your friend to *Mehmani* in America, they all started smiling. My friend Kiran Maheshwari, who was seated next to me on the podium leaned over and said, "We have the same custom in our state."

The point is that this custom was prevalent in different parts of the country, and still is. But the word used for it varies according to the language spoken in an area. In the villages of Bihar, before a girl's wedding, she is invited to every house in the village for *Mehmani*, caste no bar. One can guess that there must have been two thoughts behind this. First, that a daughter does not belong to a particular caste. A daughter belongs to the entire village. Before she leaves for her in-laws' house, families from all castes bid her farewell. The second thought is that villages had the practice of untouchability. An unmarried girl used to not have a particular caste. After the wedding, she would belong to a particular caste and would not be allowed to share meals with people of other castes. So *Mehmani* was a way to allow her to have a last meal with people of other castes before getting married. Untouchability and caste system became a curse for our society over time, but the concepts must have originated to fulfil some substantial goals for the betterment of our social system.

Anyhow, right now I do not want to get into the pros and cons of the caste system. I am reminded right now of those social customs that even we have stopped following after coming to live in the cities. There is a trend in the educated women of my generation (who have moved from their villages to the cities) to leave or change their customs. For one, it was difficult to continue following the traditions far away from their villages, living amongst unfamiliar neighbors who had come to live in the cities from different parts of the country. Second, after settling down in the cities, the old traditions with roots in the villages seemed to reek of backwardness and we heartlessly shunned them. These days, however, I am trying to get to the roots of those customs and understanding their significance. I have had the opportunity to participate in several international conferences. Often in these conferences, while looking for solutions for a society's current problems, we come to accept international unification. It is believed that the social problems faced by different countries of the world—USA, England, South Africa, India, and China, are all the same, and that the same measures can be used to find their solutions. My thinking is slightly different in this area. In looking for solutions for those problems, I often look towards our villages. Did these problems exist fifty-sixty years ago (as far back as I can see)? If they did exist, how did people solve those problems back then? It is true that society has changed, conditions have changed, the environment has changed. So, an old medicine may not work for a new disease. Even so, the lessons can only be learnt from our own history.

So, one international conference I attended was on the topic of "nutrition for expecting mothers." Before my speech in that conference, I started thinking—how did our society deal with this issue? There was no radio or television in those days, then how did they bring about awareness? I came across one custom. In our villages, an expecting mother's relatives used to send her copious amounts of delicacies, sweets, and other nutritious food so that she could continue using them for a while. You might remember when your Sangita *bhabhi* (sister-in-law) was pregnant, her mother (who lived in Delhi) used to send *puri* (puffed fried bread) stuffed with lentils, *kheer* (rice pudding), *pua* (type of sweet), vegetables and a lot of other nutritious foods for her. We used to enjoy those delicacies too. In our village, this food basket sent for the pregnant woman used to be known as *Saghor*. This custom was followed in other parts of the country too with a different name everywhere.

I included this information in my speech in that international conference and added that, in our villages, every child used to be considered a social treasure and resource. That's why it used to be the society's responsibility to make sure the child was born healthy and it is too. Women facing poverty also had to go through pregnancy. So, this mindset was developed in the society that a pregnant woman should be provided whatever she wishes to eat, even if it meant taking away from someone else's share, otherwise the baby born to her would keep drooling. Never mind if there is no scientific link found between the diet of a pregnant woman and her baby's drooling, but this mindset ensured that a pregnant woman had a nutritious diet.

Not only that, the folksongs sung at the time of a baby's birth (*Sohar*) were also a great source of information for women on what to eat, what not to eat, and how to stay healthy during and after pregnancy.

Just think. How songs, rituals, and stories were used as a medium to educate women and to communicate the do's and don'ts of pregnancy. These days, even in India, a lot of money is being spent on information and awareness campaigns. However, these campaigns do not have an impact as deep as the costless folksongs and rituals used to have.

I know when your friends are expecting, you will invite them for *Saghor.* I like to hear these things also because this way our newer generations, whether living in India or abroad, come to learn about our culture and traditions. Traditions are not a burden. They are not just something you must do. Some traditions are lost with time, and some should be left behind. However, most traditions and customs have a deep purpose. We should certainly ponder over them. We should follow them to whatever extent possible. Life is a relay race. Life lessons learnt from your mother should continue to be taught to your daughter, and so on.

When your nephews Dhruv and Dheer were born (in America), I was there both times and completed the rituals related to childbirth (*Chhathi pooja*, celebration on the sixth day after birth). You sang *Sohar* (folksongs about childbirth). I asked you to apply kohl to the newborns (a ritual) which is performed by the aunt, and told you to ask your brother, sister-in-law, and even your father for money in return (also a part of the ritual). At the time of Dheer's ceremony, you said, "Mom, why should I ask, no one really gives any money!"

I said, "How can you say they don't give? Everyone gives you something or the other. Actually, in these rituals, there is more fun in demanding the money than in receiving it." New mothers who do not have a sister-in-law miss having one on occasions like these. The new fathers, too, feel the lack of a sister.

Indian society has kept all the relationships bound together by some tradition, custom, or festival. At the time of those festivals, the absence of that particular relationship in your life hurts a lot. This way, different family members and people from all sections of the society are given important roles at various life events—wedding, childbirth, etc. All life events are festivals. What can you say about a society where death is also a festival?

But I feel sad that our new generations are deprived of these festivals. People are finding new ways to find happiness, but those new ways do not connect people with people. The truth is that people want to find happiness while living their own lives—which is never possible. Happiness is found in living for others—whether it is only for a few moments or for a lifetime.

I am reminded of an incident from my childhood. My brother was ill with smallpox. My father used to go to the town every day (from the village) for work. One evening I asked him eagerly, "Dad, there is an exhibition in town. Will you take us there?"

He said, "These days I don't notice anything around me while going back and forth from the office. I go with my eyes shut and return the same way. Your brother is sick. My attention is focused on him alone."

That day I realized that our father used to love my brother very much. My young mind was influenced a lot by that incident. I got a lesson too on how to behave with a child. How much we learn from these small things! A lot more compared to reading fat books of scriptures. The education provided in schools and colleges makes engineers and doctors—the education that brings livelihood. On the other hand, the education provided by these customs and rituals related to relationships helps us live a smooth and sweet life. The main lesson is to make your life blessed by living for others.

Now you will say, "Mom, that's enough. You just keep on talking."

I am not talking. I am writing. If I talk, only you will hear, but if I write, many other daughters, daughters-in-law, and mothers will read. In fact, I really want the mothers to read these letters and want to remind them to definitely teach their daughters everything they learned from their mothers. Now our daughters are becoming mothers too, so I want those daughters to read the letters as well. You used to complain often, "Mom, how many daughters do you have! Uma Bharti, Poornima Advani, and so many others (younger women colleagues). Then why will you care only about me?"

It was a fair complaint. But what can I do? It is true, I have many daughters. I enjoy giving them love and receiving their respect. But that does not lessen my love for you. You are you after all and all my other daughters love you too. Your share of love keeps growing. Now you too are sharing your love. That is why you will never be lacking in love. The more you share, the more you will get. Our time, resources, and love—they don't dissipate by sharing, they grow.

Your Mom

□

Women's Role in the Development of Hindi

Dear daughter Mili,

Always stay happy!

I trust you are attending to your studies with all your heart. Now your course is coming to an end. I remember I had visited London to participate in the Sixth World Hindi Conference. After spending just two days there, I left for America to visit you. It had only been two months since you had joined Cornell University for higher studies. I was very worried when I visited you. How will you endure for four years? The four years are now over and we did not even realize it.

The Seventh World Hindi Conference will be held in Suriname. I am planning to attend that too. During the sixth conference, while sharing my thoughts on the expansion of Hindi, I had mentioned that two of my children are in America. They scored high in all their written and oral exams in English. I am happy about that. People congratulate me for your success too. I accept the wishes for your accomplishments. But you know that I cannot take credit for your command of the English language. Until now, I have not said even one complete sentence in English to my children. It is not that I do not know English. I do not have anything against the language either. But it is a fact that I am comfortable talking with my children in

Hindi. While educating my children in Delhi's schools, I never felt the need to speak with them in English.

Your brother has been in America for thirteen years now, and you for four years. Neither I nor you two ever felt the need to converse with me in English. I know a family that has been living in America for the last thirty-five years. Their children were born and raised there. They speak in Bhojpuri at home. You will find people outside India who speak different Indian languages—Gujrati, Marathi, Bangla, etc. Not all, but many people try to speak only in their mother tongue with their people.

In fact, a mother tongue feels like a mother's embrace. It brings peace and calm to the mind. One does not need to be extra cautious when speaking in their mother tongue. There is one saying in Bihar—"When I find river Ganga, I will dive in to bathe; when I find my mother, I will talk my heart out." The way you can talk with your mother openly, the same way a mother tongue provides ease and openness. Certainly, a mother tongue is the first language a mother teaches to her child. One specialty of the Indian culture is that we call the river Ganga, the holy book Gita, as well as a cow our mother. A language that is akin to a mother is indeed the mother tongue.

The language that flows down a baby's throat along with the mother's milk, is certainly taught by the mother. A mother will nourish and nurture the language as she nurtures her baby. This is why mothers have a key role to play in the development of a mother tongue. A mother tongue will be the language of the heart. Any language can be the language of the stomach (a language that helps us earn a living and feed ourselves); in fact, there can be many languages for the stomach. But the stomach is different from the heart. Both are needed to keep a person alive. It is the mother who teaches the language of the heart and keeps it flowing from one generation to another—like the waters in river Ganga. It is not necessary that the language of the father's stomach is the same as that of the son's stomach.

While the father may earn an income based on the English language, his son may need to learn French or German to earn a living. However, the language of the heart that flows from one generation to the next will always be the same.

Experience tells us that when a child reaches her mother's age, she becomes her reflection. May be not so much in a physical way, but a child's language is influenced in a big way by the mother. Children often get annoyed when mothers use idioms or sayings or repeat lines from folk songs in conversations. But when they grow up, the children start including them in their way of talking. They use them to clarify or explain their points. This is how the sayings, idioms, and phrases that are vital to the enrichment and expansion of a language have continued flowing through the generations, even if they are not written down anywhere. This important task is fulfilled in a special way by the mothers.

It is worrisome that new-age mothers in the cities have started teaching their babies the language of the stomach. Leaving the rich vocabulary of their mother tongue Hindi, mothers want their babies to learn words from the English language. They are afraid that if those words do not float on the tongues of their darlings, then they may not get into good (English-medium) schools. So, the children learn their A, B, Cs and One, Two, Three's much before they learn the Hindi alphabet.

I am reminded of your childhood. Your father was a professor of English. But in the house, we never spoke to each other in English even by mistake. Before sending you to school, I started teaching you the Hindi alphabet. You started learning very fast, even writing early. I completed a novel in six months and by the age of four you started reading and writing complex Hindi sentences like, "*Dilli Bharat varsh ki rajdhani hai*" (Delhi is the capital of India). You began learning English after starting school. I believe that because of your strong base in the Hindi language, you did not have much difficulty learning

English. Not only that, during our daily strolls in the park and while traveling, I made you memorize couplets and songs by *Rahim, Kabir, Tulsidas,* and *Meera.* You got used to it. As soon as we would sit on a rickshaw or in a train to go somewhere, you would start repeating those couplets and songs.

I believe that your language was enriched by soaking your throat and tongue from an early age in these nectar-droplets from the Hindi literature and your behavior and thinking became more advanced as compared to your peer group. This is the importance of informal education.

I feel that every mother should realize that it is her responsibility to generate a love for their own language in her children. Last year in America, I was pleased to watch you speak in Hindi with your fellow Indian students. Many years ago, I had visited Mauritius. A resident of that country was talking to me in English. A third person was listening. I mentioned during the conversation that I was from Bihar.

That third person immediately asked (in Bhojpuri, a language spoken in the state of Bihar), "You are from Bihar? Do you speak Bhojpuri?"

I said, in Bhojpuri, "I know, understand and speak Bhojpuri."

Then that person started scolding the first person from his country (in Bhojpuri), "She knows Bhojpuri, then why are you chit-chatting with her in English?" Then we started talking in Bhojpuri. A fifteen-minute conversation with me was aired on television. I spoke in Bhojpuri throughout. That was it. Wherever I went, people would feel delighted knowing that I was from the land of their ancestors. Indians who went to other countries in the form of bonded labor 150-200 years ago have kept their mother tongues alive in those countries. No language can stay alive by itself. With it are assimilated the rituals, customs, and religious activities of that society. In fact, every language has its own environment where it roams freely, grows, and expands. It keeps evolving and taking newer forms despite growing old. If you keep a language alive, the entire culture stays alive. A mother is the main driver of culture. Our culture is where a mother is worshipped, and in the same sense, a language is considered a mother—a mother has been given the responsibility to teach that a language is a mother too. A mother tongue is also to be worshipped.

Other Indian languages have also been helpful in the expansion of Hindi. Sanskrit is the mother of all these languages. In today's age of computers, it has become easier for Hindi to travel, expand, and thrive in the world. There are more special and better conditions now for Hindi to develop. Many factors are complementary while others are competitive—both set of conditions are required for the growth of any language. The script of every language serves a complementary role in its development. There are great opportunities now for the development of the Hindi script. In all of Asia, India has the largest numbers of English speakers. However, while sixty crore (six million) people speak-read-write Hindi, a hundred crore (ten million) people are able to understand Hindi. Even now Hindi is lagging in the fields of science and technology, and special attention needs to be paid there. But Hindi is getting special attention in the fields of business and advertisement. Hindi magazines have grown in number. Even in the southern states (non-Hindi speaking), Hindi magazines are published and read. But English has a greater influence there. Hindi cinema has certainly played a big role in the expansion of Hindi worldwide. Doordarshan (Indian public television) has played a special role as well.

Indian music has an expansive space. It is liked by people all over the world. There is a lot of variation in Indian music. We can use this medium to have the world taste the different flavors of our language.

These factors complete Hindi. However, its competitor English has also played a special role in the development of Hindi. English has entered every household. Mothers are teaching English, the language of the stomach, so their children have an easier time finding jobs. This is unfortunate. A mother is the ruler of hearts—at least she should be teaching the language of the heart.

In the coming years, there will be no shortage of Indian mothers in the world. Just think. Thousands of girls your age have gone to America. They should try to speak their own language at home. Hindi should be the language at home, no matter what language is used at work. Women living outside India can make Hindi a language spoken worldwide. When our girls can convince foreign boys to get married according to Indian customs, then why not to speak their language at home? At least Indian couples should speak in Hindi at home. You young boys and girls should make Hindi the language of romance, and the other (non-Indian) youth will understand it. They will be enamored by your love song. They will want to read Hindi literature. Hindi is a language of love.

You boys and girls living abroad should learn to love yourselves. Inherent in you is your country, and the Indian language, food, and clothing. Appreciate the diversity of the Hindi language. Acknowledge that in our society, every relation has a specific name—*chacha* (father's brother*), mama* (mother's brother), *mausa* (mother's sister's husband). They are not all "uncles" like it is in the English language. Similarly, every aunt has a specific name in Hindi, *mausi* (mother's sister), *chachi* (father's brother's wife), *bua* (father's sister). Do you know what is special about the Hindi alphabet?—what we write is what we read. This is not the case in English where you write something and read something else. There are many other specialties of the Hindi language. Unless you are aware of those qualities, you will not feel proud of your language. You will not use it to connect with others. In fact, through you, I want to make these points to other Indians too. To women who live in India and those who live outside India. When a home's decoration, upkeep, and taste of the food is determined by the woman, then why not the language? If we make up our minds, Hindi will be the language of our homes.

I am happy that you follow this. Your brother, despite having lived in America for thirteen years now, in conversations with me uses all the idioms and sayings that he learnt while playing in my lap. The fact that you earn dollars in America does not give me as much happiness as your effort to protect and spread your land's voice and essence.

My blessings and wishes are with you in your effort.

Your Mom

□

Moisture of the Soil

Dear Mili,

Blessings!

I know that these days you are waiting for interview calls from universities where you have applied for faculty positions. It is one thing for children to go to a foreign land to study, but once they start working there it means they will settle down in that place. In a way the whole world is our own. A person can come and go wherever he or she wishes to. People have always been traveling from one corner of the world to another in search of a livelihood. But your own country is your own. A country is not just its forests, rivers, and houses. There is a life force that flows in it. A foreign land is different indeed. But even within a country, different regions have different flows of emotions that render a special identity to each place.

The fifth day of Margashirsh (a month of the Hindu calendar) is also known as *Vivah Panchami* (*Vivah* means wedding, *Panchami* means fifth day). It is believed that Sita and Rama got married on this day. Every year on this day, episodes from the Sita-Ram wedding are enacted very religiously in Janakpur (the ancient Indian city where Sita was from). This year too Rama's wedding procession traveled from Ayodhya (Rama's kingdom) to Janakpur, where the wedding of Sita and Rama took place. I too participated in this wedding procession along with fifteen other women. On the way, we also visited *Ahilya Sthan* (Ahilya's place). Ahilya's episode is an important one in Rama's story. The story goes like this. Ahilya's husband, Saint Gautam, witnesses her in a suspicious state with another man and he places a curse on her to become a rock. When in the Treta Yuga (the second of the four ages in Hinduism), Rama and Laxman (brothers) travel to Janakpur with their Guru Vishwamitra, they meet Ahilya in the form of a rock. The rock transforms into a beautiful woman when Rama's foot touches it. There is a temple in that place to this date.

In that village of Mithilanchal (a region in eastern India), there are many educated scholars. When you hear them tell Sita's story, you feel as if the entire Mithilanchal region is still in pain because of the tragedies Sita, a daughter of this land, suffered in her lifetime. Their belief is that Mithilanchal's daughter Sita did not experience happiness in her life. Sita's father Janak had taken a vow to wed his daughter Sita to the man who could overpower Shiva's divine bow–Rama broke the bow and married Sita. Rama was about to be coronated. But he had to leave for the forest to obey his father's orders. Sita expresses her desire to accompany him to the forest. Rama warns her of the discomforts of a forest and says, "You are very delicate. The forest life will be very hard. So, you should stay in Ayodhya and take care of my parents."

But Sita reminds him of her duty as a wife and says that she will happily suffer all hardships along with her husband. She goes to the forest with Rama and Laxman. She suffers a lot along the way. King Janak's daughter and King Dashrath's daughter-in-law who is used to living in palaces goes to the forest in bare feet and in plain clothes. She does not complain about the hardships she faces in the forest. Her character is the epitome of patience and perseverance. During the time they live in Panchvati, Sita gets kidnapped by Ravana (the king of Lanka). Ravana keeps her in Ashoka Vatika (a garden in Ravana's kingdom). Rama and Ravana wage a battle in which Ravana dies. Sita reunites with Rama. But because she lived in Ravana's kingdom, she has to pass the *agni pareeksha* (the fire test) to prove her purity. She passes the test. Rama returns to his kingdom after a fourteen-year exile in the forest and his coronation is celebrated. He becomes the king. Sita gets pregnant. And hearing a washerman speak disparagingly about Sita, Rama abandons Sita. He sends her to live in Saint Valmiki's *ashram* (hermitage). Sita gives birth to twin boys, Luv and Kush, in the Valmiki *ashram*. She raises her boys there and teaches them everything a prince should know. When they become young men, Rama conducts his *Ashwamedh Yagya* (a horse sacrifice ritual performed by kings).

Luv and Kush capture the horse that was released in Ayodhya for Rama's *Ashwamedh Yagya*. The boys fight Rama's army. After the army chief Shatrughna gets injured, Rama himself comes to the Valmiki *ashram*. There he faces Sita. He finds out that the fearless boys are his sons and embraces them. Rama's eyes reflect his plea for forgiveness, but Sita does not say a word. She does not complain. The earth splits open and Sita vanishes into it.

This is Rama's tale in short. It shows the greatness and grandness of Sita's personality, along with Rama's. In our culture, Rama is the ideal man—an epitome of dignity, conduct, and righteousness. Rama established the code of conduct in our family and social life. But sometimes when you think about it, you might feel that Sita was ahead of Rama in this area. Her courage, patience, knowledge, and capability were no less than that of Rama. She was a righteous woman. That's why she accompanied Rama to the forest to fulfill her duty as a wife. Both Rama and Kaushalya (his mother) had tried to dissuade her. But she convinced them by her knowledge, wisdom, and wit. She told them about the duties of a wife. She endured hardship in the forest with Rama without so much as a complaint. Even in Ravana's Ashoka Vatika, she waited patiently. On Rama's request, she went through the *agni-pareeksha* (fire test). Even after getting banished from Ayodhya, she continued fulfilling her duties as a wife and a mother. While living in a saint's *ashram*, she gave the appropriate training to her sons on how to become kings. It was her ambition to instill in her sons the qualities needed to become a good citizen and a good king.

A life like Sita's cannot be lived without infallible courage. Therefore, Sita is an ideal not only for the Indian women, but for women all over the world.

It is surprising that Sita is still alive in the land of Mithilanchal. Hundreds of thousands of people had assembled to welcome the wedding procession. As if they were truly watching Rama's wedding procession. Their eyes were moist, voices were full of compassion.

Blessed is this land and blessed is our *sanskriti* (culture). Kids going to foreign lands are earning in dollars. Their lives are full of comfort and luxury. No obstacles or pain. But I feel that they are deprived of their soil's moisture and aroma. Sita is the daughter of the entire Mithilanchal region. But you are also a daughter of Matihani (our village in Bihar), are you not? You might remember—on one of your trips to the village, a woman who had never seen you before, had said joyfully, "This is our Mili. Our Mili!" She is proud of her village and of the daughters of her village—this is how it is with your own village and your daughters. This is why the daughter of *Treta Yug* (the age of Treta), Janak's precious daughter Sita, is still the daughter of Mithilanchal.

I tell you stories of our historic and mythical women characters so that you are able to understand our culture. So that you can share these stories with your friends in America.

This is not my indirect attempt to convince you to return to India, but a way to make you feel proud of your culture by knowing our history. Our children who have left India have not gone only with technical knowledge, they have also taken with them the essence and capability of a very ancient human civilization. I wish these children had been told their history in this form.

With Blessings,
Your Mom

□

Daughter is a Father's Strength

Darling daughter Mili,

Always stay happy!

Last month you travelled to Switzerland. For over a month you were busy with preparing the papers you were going to present in an international students' conference. You planned to focus on other things once the conference was over. There were many things we wanted to draw your attention towards, but we had postponed doing that too. We decided to wait and broach those subjects after you were done participating in the conference.

The other day you called us from Switzerland. We had been a little worried. You were traveling alone to Europe from America (Cornell University) for the first time. You had also traveled to New York city for a day to get the visa. We were receiving timely updates. Sometimes I think how different the world is now in some matters. After graduating the eleventh grade, I had requested of my father to enroll me in college. I was the first girl in my village to pass the matriculation examination (tenth grade). My father was proud. He did not have the financial means to send me to a boarding college, but he still managed to gather resources to do so. Only because he wanted to encourage his daughter. We too did not have the means to send you to America for higher studies. But with your brother Praveen's encouragement and consultation, as well as with your intelligence and hard work, you managed to get a scholarship at Cornell University. You have been living there on your own for four years now. You are certainly more confident now. In India, especially in the state of Bihar, even now the conditions are such that a girl cannot travel alone from one place to another.

You called from Switzerland and told us that your paper presentation was very well received. I doubt anyone else was as happy as your father on hearing this news. Everyone was happy—your brothers, sisters-in-law, your little nieces, and I. Your uncles, Ashwiniji and Jagdeesh Mathurji, were also pleased. But a father's happiness on his daughter's accomplishment has a very different flavor. I was reminded of the times when my father used to get excited when the results of my tenth, twelfth, bachelors, and master's exams were released. He would make offerings to Gods, hold a *Satyanarayan Katha* (prayers) at home, and do many other gatherings to create opportunities to tell the villagers how special his daughter was. I had only one goal, to study religiously—to make my father happy. His happiness was my motivation. Your father retold many times all the comments you received after presenting your paper. It is a good thing that he was the one to speak directly with you on the phone. Otherwise, he would have given me a hard time with his barrage of questions—"What was the comment? Who said that? And?..."

The results of your twelfth-grade exams had been released. Your father called from Bihar to ask about your grades. I started singing lines from a folk song from Bihar known as *"sohar"* which is sung when a baby is born, "The womb that gave birth to this child should be engraved in gold."

You had received better grades than both your brothers. But the folk songs sung in the villages have always been discriminating between girls and boys. The truth is that in these *sohar* songs, never is a girl born, only boys. Even when a girl is born, she is considered a curse. A daughter's parents curse their bad luck. A womb that carries a girl is blamed and many rituals and customs make a girl child feel like a burden.

These days in India, girls are getting excellent grades in many examinations. They are given the opportunity to excel. They are investing all their energy in getting an education. This is a good thing. This is why society's outlook towards daughters is changing too. How much the society has changed! Thousands of girls like you are going abroad to study. After your phone call, the words your father uttered were, "now it's done." I could feel his satisfaction in these three words. Parents have an important role in educating their children and making them qualified, and the children's accomplishments give support and strength to the parents in their old age. In fact, parents find joy in seeing their children make progress, earning respect in society, and having a more comfortable lifestyle than themselves. They do not require the children to provide to them as much comfort and luxury as they have in their own lives.

All these expectations used to be with sons previously. Sons were expected to provide support and safety to the parents in their old age. Daughters were supposed to leave for their in-laws' house, and they were raised accordingly. At the same time, parents did not expect to get anything in return from daughters. Things are different now. Daughters, too, take care of aging parents, and parents are agreeing to get support from daughters when they grow old. Many things will change in the society just with this one change. Daughters are very dear to their fathers. They make their fathers proud with their good deeds and accomplishments. You may remember, your father used to tell you time and again when you were little, "Become an intellectual!"

Your father did not like to see you dressing up in jewelry, fancy clothes, or makeup. "Become an intellectual!" he used to say. You would reply, "Yes, yes, Papa! I will become an intellectual!" May be that's why he uttered the words, "Now it's done." This meant that his job was done. His daughter was recognized.

A mother and a father are different. Your accomplishments

also make me happy. But my mind is more focused on your marriage, household, and family life. I worry about those things. These big accomplishments are very important in life, but for us women, our household accomplishments bring us greater joy. A woman makes a home.

When I got married, I did not know how to run a household at all. I studied at a boarding school. Your father used to complain jokingly to my father, "Girls should not be sent to boarding school. They do not get trained in running a household."

My father would understand his problems, but he used to say, "Let her complete her master's degree. She will eventually learn how to manage a household." And that's what happened.

For the time being, congratulations on your success and best wishes for your future!

Your Mom

□

The Unwritten Constitution

Dear Mili,

Blessings!

I hope you are doing well. In a previous letter, I had written to you about Nal-Damyanti's story. I trust that you are giving some thought to that story. Damyanti's character is truly one to emulate. She was so brave and practical. In fact, these qualities are present in every woman to some extent. That is why daughters are special, just like you are. Last week you had an exam. Since childhood, you have always been unduly nervous before an exam. You would prepare very seriously for every exam, but on seeing me you would say, "Mom, I am definitely going to fail this time." And every time you got the best grades. Even from America, you repeat the same thing on the phone before an exam, "Mom, I am going to fail!" I can feel your nervousness each time.

But I am always sure that you will never be unsuccessful. Because a person who takes his or her responsibilities seriously rarely fails in life. One more thing. Your father would always say on seeing you study all the time, "Mili, don't study so much. Specially not on the day before the exam."

But when did you ever pay heed? Last week you informed your sister-in-law on the phone, "Please tell Mom I have had some yogurt. I also put a little dot of yogurt on my forehead. Now I am going for my interview."

Sangita (your sister-in-law) informed me of this when I

returned from my trip to Patna. I was pleased to hear that even in America, you followed the Indian custom of putting a dot of yogurt on the forehead to make your journey successful. This is how the *sanskaars* (values) given in childhood become part of a person's lifestyle.

How does eating yogurt and putting some on your forehead help answer the exam questions, if at all, I have not been able to understand to date. Is there a scientific basis to this? No one has ever told me nor have I been curious to know. It was certainly the case that before I left the house to take an exam, my mother would be standing with a bowl of yogurt in her hand. After putting a dot on my forehead, she would put a spoonful of yogurt in my mouth. I would touch her feet (to take blessings) and leave the house. She would say, "May Brahma and Vishnu protect you, and Ganesha always be with you." Father would say, "May your journey be auspicious."

After hearing their wishes, certainly the fear of the exam eased a little. While answering the questions, this thought used to come to mind, "I prayed to the Gods. Also took the blessings of mother and father. The answers will come easily to me. The results with definitely be good."

It was the final exams for my master's course. For some reason, there was a long gap between the last two exams. I was going to give the exam for the last subject twenty days after the previous exam. My mother had already returned to the village. While entering the examination hall, I remembered—I had not put a dot of yogurt on my forehead. And that was it. I lost my confidence. I scored well in that subject as well, but even to this date I feel that I could have received a better score. It is all about the confidence of your mind. And our success, failure, gain, loss, are also based on the science of the mind.

My mother was not educated. But she understood the importance of education. That is why she took special care of me during my exam days. From taking care of my food, rest, studying to placing a dot of yogurt on my forehead before leaving for an exam. I repeated the same things with my children. I believe that my children will continue these ways with their children as I did to them.

The truth is that no one really knows the reasons behind these rituals and customs. People just repeat the behaviors of their parents with their children.

These *sanskaars* are passed on primarily by mothers. While my father used to be present on the porch, it was my mother who used to place the yogurt dot on my forehead. Not my father. Your father did not do it either.

It is the woman's responsibility to give the *sanskaars.* Today in our society, these small things that are actually big for a disciplined life, are being abandoned mindlessly. If it's useless to follow customs without understanding them, then it is also damaging to abandon them without understanding them. Children usually make fun of mothers feeding them yogurt before the exams. The truth is that even mothers have discontinued such customs and rituals thinking they are orthodox and hypocritical. Last month a boy from our village, Dipu, came to work in our house. Samridhi (your niece) had her books spread all over the floor. Dipu picked them up and touched them to his forehead. Samridhi started laughing, "Why did you touch the books with your forehead?" He said, "*Vidya is a Devi* (knowledge is a Goddess). We should never let our feet touch the books. We should pay our respect to the books by touching them to our foreheads."

Dipu is educated. But he did not learn to behave like this from his teacher. He learnt this by observing other villagers. Without giving it a thought, he behaves the way the villagers behave. Now Samridhi too has learnt it from him. You have remembered the things you were taught in your childhood. You have included them in your behaviors. That is a good thing. I hope you will teach them to your children as well.

The society operates on an unwritten constitution. There are many such behaviors in our daily lives that we have not read in the books. We saw others do these things, and we made them a part of our lives. But now when I think about it, I realize that these rituals certainly have their reasons. My mother did not put turmeric in our evening meals. When I asked why, she told me, "This is how it is. Turmeric should not be ground at night." She did not know the reason why turmeric was not ground at night. But I figured out a reason after thinking over it. Turmeric root can have insects. There was no electricity in the villages. People used to grind turmeric on a stone. Since they would miss any insects inside the turmeric root in the dark, it became a tradition that people would not grind turmeric after it was dark. Now people buy turmeric powder, so this tradition is no longer relevant. I was curious to know the reason behind the tradition, and the answer I found seems convincing. My mother did not even ask what the reason was.

I believe that these superstitions definitely have a reason behind them. Feeding yogurt and placing a yogurt dot on the forehead can also be reasoned. It was probably done with a goal to keep the student's mind and body cool during an exam. It is important, after all, to have a calm mind when writing an exam.

Whatever the reason, I am satisfied that you remember the things I taught you even after going so far away. You try to follow the customs. You do not have the desire to abandon Indian customs and rituals and adopt an American lifestyle without any thought. No one society has all good traditions, nor does any one society have all the bad traditions. Every society has some traditions that are worth adopting, and some worth abandoning.

I hope your interview went very well. After all you went with a yogurt dot on your head.

With best wishes,
Your Mom

□

A Daughter's Father

Dear daughter Mili,

Blessings!

Early this morning your father started crying again while watching a movie on Doordarshan (Indian public television). He cried a lot. The movie was on the relationship between a father and a daughter. The daughter brings a new life to her father. She cajoles, cries, gets upset, scorns, pampers—does all she can to bring her father on the right path. The father gives up drinking to fulfil his daughter's wish. He begins singing songs. In the end, the daughter says, "I am proud of you, Papa."

The movie ends with the father and the daughter restoring their trust in each other. These days we wake up around four or four-thirty in the morning. They show good movies on DD Metro (one of the public channels on TV). Usually, we are only able to watch a quarter or half of a movie. But we like it a lot. The fact is that the storylines of these movies are connected to life. During the day where is the time to watch movies? Its work, work, work!

Every morning your father becomes troubled by watching such movies. His eyes tear up and sometimes even spill over. Who knows how this notion developed in society that men are hard-hearted and women are soft and emotional? The truth is that men and women are not very different in these matters. Your grandmother often used to say, "My son (your father) has a wooden heart. He will not cry even when I die."

I think she was so wrong about her son. Then I think maybe she was right. A mother often feels that her child does not care about her feelings. In fact, parents expect too much from their children. Children are just children. They do not meet their parents' expectations at that time. But it is not the case that they do not listen to their parents. They do listen and internalize too. But they are so carefree in front of parents that they keep refusing to follow their orders. The relationship between parents and children is like a coconut—hard on the outside, soft and loving on the inside.

Compared to a son, a daughter understands a father's sentiments better. Nature has provided daughters some special powers such that even at a young age they are able to understand their father's emotions. They respect the emotions too.

It is also true that even young girls have maternal emotions in them. This is why your nieces, Hansa and Samridhi, are able to understand their father's emotions. When I had to leave the house for a period of time, your Nawin *bhaiya* (elder brother) said, "Who will love me now? My mother has left."

Six-year-old Samridhi said to him, "Papa, I am here for you. Now I am your mother. Play 'mom-mom' with me."

And then she became her father's mom, took his head in her lap and kept caressing it. My son would sometimes pretend to cry for me. She would console him. Daughters do take better care of their fathers. In fact, every wife becomes her husband's mother after a few years of marriage and starts taking special care of his likes-dislikes, comfort, and happiness. She starts feeling motherly towards her husband as well.

Women have these natural abilities, but the family and society also keep finding ways to develop those qualities. Therefore, generation after generation, women have kept winning hearts on the basis of their motherliness and service towards others. They have received respect in return. There are very few exceptions to this.

But these days girls are under so much pressure to study and make a career that they are becoming deprived of the joy one receives by serving others.

A few days ago, you told me that on the occasion of Holi (festival of colors) this year, you had made several Indian delicacies—*pua* (fried pancakes), *kheer* (rice pudding), and *dahi-vada* (yogurt-soaked-fritters). Along with your friends, you also invited an Indian boy who joined your university a year ago. You served him food and also kept offering him more food to eat. You told me that he teared up while eating. You asked him jokingly, "What's the matter? Why are you crying? Is the *kheer* (rice pudding) too spicy?"

He did not laugh at your joke. He wiped his tears. Calming himself, he said, "After coming here, no one has offered me extra servings like this. Throughout the year, I have been cooking for myself—sometimes I eat and sometimes I go to bed without eating. No one bothers to ask me if I have eaten. Today when you served me food, and kept offering more, I was reminded of my mother in India. My mother must have made the same delicacies for Holi. I know that she must not have been able to eat them herself. Because I am not there. She must have cried even on the day of a festival. I will write to her that I found a mother in America." He laughed a little while saying the last sentence.

I know you must have found it intolerable to be taken as a mother by him. You must have also been upset with him. But after he left, you must have realized that that moment gave you happiness. You must have felt gratified. You said to him, "Stop it! I am not your mother. I am never going to invite you again, never going to serve you any food." But I know that you will invite him. You will serve him food again and even offer more servings. On this Holi, his tears drenched you in their colors. You will want to play Holi with those colors next year too.

Dear, it brings us joy to spend our time and resources in the service of others. That's why a woman stays happy even when she does not have any comforts. She keeps distributing such things even from her empty home that do not require any vessels for storage. They are emotions that cannot be seen. But even the most ordinary woman distributes these emotions of her heart by filling up the vessels in her eyes. Even after doling out the emotions continuously, she does not become empty, she keeps getting refilled. Does a river ever notice when a pot of water is taken out of it? No, right? There is no emptiness there too. There should not be a sign of emptiness in a woman either. Take a handful from the *sanskriti* (culture), it does not lessen, it keeps expanding.

In India, a person's life is knitted with the yarn of relationships, a yarn that has many colors and many levels of warmth.

A father-daughter relationship is indeed unique. It is wonderful. Despite giving birth to the daughter and keeping her close to herself, a mother is not able to make the daughter her own. She belongs to her father. A woman gives her husband a big gift in the form of a daughter. In front of a daughter, even the man with the cruelest heart melts. A daughter starts caring so much for her father since a very young age that she leaves the mother behind. Both father and daughter revel in each-other's company.

In our region, Mithilanchal, many songs are sung during a daughter's wedding. All songs invoke the emotions associated with the daughter's relationships with her parents, with her siblings, with the villagers, and even with the farm animals. One song on the father-daughter relationship describes how the father is worried on seeing that his daughter is of marriageable age. How will he do *kanyadaan* (the gift of a daughter)? How will he get separated from a piece of his heart? One more thing I want to point out is that in these songs from the Mithilanchal region, all brides-to-be are Sita and all fathers are Janak (Sita's father in Ramayana). The condition of a bride's father's heart is described in reference to King Janak. This too is a specialty of our *sanskriti*.

What an irony it is! A father finds a groom for his daughter, makes arrangements for the wedding, and when the time comes to bid farewell to his daughter, his heart becomes very weak. There is hardly any other social occasion that involves such a combination of joy and sadness. The bride's father feels proud upon gifting his daughter but remains very humble in front of his son-in-law and his family. Why so? He treats his son-in-law like God. Perhaps because he wants to make sure his daughter does not suffer, that she gets respect in her in-laws' home. Even while raising you in Delhi, I taught you all the folksongs from Bihar. These are *sanskaar* (culture; way of life) songs. Schools and colleges teach how to become doctors and engineers, but these folksongs teach the art of maintaining the various relationships in family life.

One folksong says, "Father, do not cut the *neem* tree, a bird has her home on it. Do not give any pain to the daughter. A daughter is like a bird. She will fly away to her in-laws' house. The *neem* tree will be left alone." There are innumerable such songs, poems, and stories that describe this emotion of a daughter's status in her father's house. The society's mindset is developed by the folk literature that exists in all customs and rituals. A daughter is considered someone else's property. She is raised with this emotion. She is cared for and she is educated with this in mind. True, this is very hard for a daughter's parents. The one who must be sent to someone else's house should also be raised as a piece of your own heart. You must find a suitable groom for her. Do her *kanyadaan*. The truth is that a daughter's parents are supposed to be stoic.

In our culture, the significance of *daan* (donation) has been explained. The donation of a daughter (*kanyadaan*) is considered the supreme donation. That is why people desire to have a girl even in a societal environment that is biased against girls. Some religious people have also been performing the *kanyadaan* of others' daughters. But it is also difficult for the girls to come to terms with their status in their parents' house. As they grow, they come to know the social perspective that they must leave for someone else's house. The house where they are being raised is not theirs. It is not easy to internalize this information. Parents do not make them realize this every moment, but it has been the norm in our society to make them aware of such bitter truths by way of folksongs and tales. A daughter is also called *duhita* (*du* means two; *hita* means beneficial)—the one who benefits two families.

In another folksong, a daughter asks her father why he decided to give her away but not the son, the daughter-in-law, the cattle, or other household belongings. The father says those are the house's *Laxmi* (wealth); only a daughter is one that belongs to someone else.

Just think. How the daughters must feel hearing this repeatedly. We can also say that by hearing, singing, and knowing these things, a girl becomes more practical. This is why in comparison to girls, boys are more naïve. Girls are practical. For this reason too, do not stay under the illusion that daughters and sons are equal. Daughters are special. They understand their parents' sentiments. Sons are not able to understand them for a long time.

A heart of a daughter's father, therefore, is very delicate. I feel that a man without a daughter cannot be complete. There should be one daughter for sure. Having a son is good, not having one is fine too. A son is wished for as an heir to care for land, property, and wealth, but a girl is needed to complete a heart and achieve humanity.

"Mom, what are you going on about!" you must be thinking. Think. By the time you reach my age, you will start thinking like this too. You will talk like this as well. People who know me will say, "She is exactly like her mother. She repeats the things her mother used to say." I wish for these things to be repeated. By you and even by your children. I know you are humming the folksong about the *neem* tree. Keep humming. These songs will make your life lively. They will make it flavorful.

With blessings,
Your Mom

□

The Giving and Receiving of Things

Dear daughter Mili,

Blessings!

Recently, a well-known Indian author Kusum Ansal sent me her novel, *Taapsi*. The book was in an envelope. For a few minutes I kept turning the envelope over and looking at it, and then opened it to find a book inside. I set the envelope down on the table and started flipping through the pages of the novel. I got lost in reading the introduction and the author's biography. My assistant, with the goal of helping me, threw the envelope in the wastepaper basket. The sound of the envelope dropping in the basket broke my concentration. I said, "No, do not throw away that envelope. I have to send my new novel *Atishaya* to Kusum Ansalji in that same envelope."

My assistant was startled by my request. But he did not ask any questions. Certainly, questions had come up in his mind. He must have wanted to make suggestions too, "Do we have a shortage of envelopes? We have hundreds of envelopes in all shapes and sizes. We should not be sending the novel in her envelope."

Yes, I knew that too. I am currently managing a high post at a public institution. Expenditure on paper, pen, and other stationery supplies is not a worry here. After all, this is the difference we have created between private and public wealth. I said to my assistant, "There was a custom in our village. If a person has sent you something in a utensil made of silver, brass, copper, or clay, or in a basket, that utensil or basket should not be returned empty. It must be returned with at least a little something in it. This has been the custom of the folk life. And you know well that I am a big proponent of keeping these customs alive as much as possible." Dilip (my assistant) was smiling. Reading his thoughts, I said, "You must be thinking that this must be a custom in the village, but this is not possible in the cities."

He was right in a way. But Mili, you are aware that even while living in a city like Delhi, I get tied up in the traditional social customs of our village life. I enjoy getting tied up in them. By talking to people from many other states, I found out that this custom was prevalent in every corner of the country. It is still practiced in the villages. Indian villages, despite having lost a lot, have still kept their customs close to heart. Life in the cities has changed. Social life has become scattered. That is why I cannot keep continuing the customs treasured by your *Dadi-Nani* (paternal and maternal grandmothers) in their exact forms. In fact, here in Delhi we do not have the same closeness with our neighbors. The more the houses have come closer, the more the families living in the houses have grown apart. There are more occasions to exchange gifts with each other. Gifts are typically exchanged on weddings or festivals. Sometimes one feels that our well-wishers have buried us under the burden of gifts. This is specially the case when you are in public office which can benefit many people. In this case, there is no doubt one gets tired of gifts small and big, and excess of anything should be avoided as they say.

But these gifts do not bring the same joy as did the delicacies, however little in amount, received in the village during festivals celebrated even during financial hardships. There used to be rich and poor families in the same neighborhood. There was financial inequality even amongst the four sons of the same father. But in social customs, a rich household did not burden the poor households in the neighborhood. Since Hira Singh's wife sent two fritters on their son's wedding, even ten years later, Moti Singh's wife keeps sending them only two fritters cooked on her expensive stove. Perhaps this was the reason why in the same village, families of low, medium, or high economic status could stay together. People living in shacks were not troubled by the mansions, and even from the high roof of the mansions people did not look down upon the shack-dwellers.

Now you will say, "Mom, what have I got to do with the history of your village? I am probably not even going to return to India now. I will work here (U.S.) now, get married, and my kids will be born here as well. I will not be able to teach these customs to my children because by hearing all this, they might only be able to enjoy the stories. But they will not be able to adopt them in their lifestyles. Their lives and lifestyles will be very different."

You are right. But who knows when and in which part of the world the situation may call for teaching and repeating the history of folk-life?

While remembering the process of exchanging things, I am reminded of one more social system. There was a loan system in the villages. Loan used to also be in the form of grain and had to be returned with interest after the new crop was harvested. Sometimes a loan had to be returned the very next month, for example, a loan taken in *Kartik* (the eighth month in Hindu calendar) had to be returned in double after the crop was harvested in *Agahan* (the ninth month). There were two other ways of exchanging land and grains in farmer families—*badlain* and *paincha.* In both these forms of exchange, no one party had a superior hand. *Badlain* meant to give something in return (barter). Suppose someone had their field close to my house and my field was closer to their house. Then fields used to get exchanged just based on a discussion between the two parties. There was certainly some paperwork involved. But there would be no exchange of money. A land's value would change according to its qualities. This was factored into the *badlain*. In the same way, grain used to be exchanged too.

Suppose my field had a crop of *moong* (type of lentil) and my neighbor's field had *arahar* (another type of lentil). Then I could trade *arahar* for *moong.* The only thing that had to be considered was that both grains had similar values and utility. In case of any differences, the quantity of the grains being traded was adjusted.

Paincha was a pleasant and cooperative system of social life. In this system, if a family did not have a particular grain or food, they would ask the neighbors for a *paincha.* Later, when they had a new crop in their fields, they would return the same amount to them. In this system of exchange, there was no interest taken or given. It was easier that way. Whether or not to give *paincha* was up to a person to decide.

These small customs played an important role in smoothening out the financial condition of the village farmers. This is why life keeps going in villages even where there is no shop in the entire village. In fact, until fifty years ago, people in the villages only needed to buy salt and kerosene oil. Once a year, at that. The village was how a village is supposed to be. Problems can also be solved by co-living.

I asked Dilip to send my book to Kusum Anjaliji in the same envelope that came from her, but I started thinking, "A village has its customs, and a city has its own. I wonder if Kusumji will feel bad seeing her envelope returned back to her."

I am always careful that if a relative or friend has gifted me something (specially a *saree*) on a special occasion, then I do not gift the same thing back to them after some time. This act, done unintentionally, causes a lot of pain to the other person. Returning someone's dish brings pleasure but returning someone's gift is painful. In our childhood, on festivals or weddings, relatives (especially a woman's parents' side) used to send gifts (*sandesh*). The word *sandesh* became *sanes* in the Mithilanchal region. Delicacies, flattened rice, yogurt, fruits, *saree*, blouse, *bindi* (red dot sticker for the forehead—a sign of marriage), bangles, and other things used to be sent in a basket made of bamboo. *Sanes* also used to be returned. So all the sweets—*thekua, gujiya, khaja* (and others)—used to be counted. The intention being that at least five more sweets, certainly not any fewer, had to be returned to the family that sent the *sanes*. There must be a profound reason behind this custom too because all customs and rituals in rural life have some significance.

All these customs have become irrelevant now. Folk life does not exist, so how would the customs survive? Social life exists in one form or another. This give and take of things adds flavor and beauty to social life. Without it, life seems dull and lonely.

I know that now amongst your foreign friends you will also start saying, "Friends, would someone give me (some particular thing) as *paincha?*"

They will ask, "*Paincha?* What is *paincha*?" And you will explain the meaning of *paincha* and *badlain*. You are a student of economics after all. It is more important for you to know these finance related customs and rituals that have now become the economic history of rural India.

I should tell you that Kusum Ansal called me to express her happiness on receiving my book *Atishaya*. She said, "First of all, the book looks beautiful. The appearance, the design of the cover page, all are very attractive. The book itself makes a special request to be opened. The publisher too has put his heart into publishing the book."

I replied, "The publisher has not published just an author's book, but his *buaji's* (aunt's) book. We have never treated our relationship to be that of an author and a publisher. The truth is that even in other fields of life, it is my attempt to spread the essence of family relationships. It keeps happening naturally without any effort or intention. And these relationships that form naturally give me immense joy."

Kusumji said, "You have another special quality. You are a frugal person."

I understood. She was hinting at the returned envelope. I said, "No, no, there is a special reason behind that."

And it took half an hour to explain the reason to her. I told her all the things I have written in this letter to you. She was very happy hearing about these customs and systems of rural life. She said, "The people we have been thinking of as uneducated and ignorant were so practical and knowledgeable. I wish we had continued some of these traditions to keep our social and family lives interconnected."

I am reminded of another incident related to this custom *paincha.* I must tell you the story otherwise I will not be able to rest. Once I was returning to Delhi from Suriname. At Suriname's Paramaribo Airport, I had given my small plastic bottle of water to *Shri* Sachhinand Pandey. He took two sips from it and gave it back. Shortly before landing at Amsterdam Airport, he took a bottle of water from the plane and gave it to me. It is not required to carry water in international airports. Water is available everywhere on the airport. Even then, he came and gave the bottled water to me. Just think why! Certainly, drinking water from my bottle felt like taking *paincha* to him, and he returned the *paincha* thinking we may or may not meet again.

So, I carried the bottle he gave me and brought it with me to India. He had returned it with interest. No loan system asks for such a big interest, not even in *chakraviddhi byaj* (compound interest). A full bottle of water in return for two sips of water.

Who knows, maybe I will get a chance to return his *paincha* water sometime?

I know you will put down the letter after reading it halfway. It is too long. I will end it now. More later.

Your Mom

□

Wedding of an Offspring

Dear daughter Mili,

Be strong!

It has been a long time since we got a letter from you. Where are you? I know your answer will be, "We talk on the phone. Then why should I write a letter?"

No, my daughter. Speaking on the phone or reading an email does not give the same satisfaction as reading a letter. Your last letter is in my purse. I made many of my friends read it. I have read it over and over while traveling in cars, trains, or planes. Each time the letter says something new. It spills out a new emotion. Fold by fold it reveals your heart. It is not easy to write a letter. Reading a letter is even harder. The amount of care that needs to be taken with language and emotions while writing a letter, also needs to be put in while reading the letter. The focus that is needed to write a letter is also required for reading it.

I know that while writing that letter two months ago you tried to be very careful. The friend you have extolled the virtues of—you have tried to tell us he is just a friend. Yes, dear. He is just a friend of yours. I understand. I also understand the words you did not write. I am sure that in your mind he is not merely a friend. You must have evaluated his good and bad qualities for another reason as well. Maybe you are also thinking of making him your life partner. But you are not able to decide for now. It is not easy for boys and girls (young men and women are referred to as boys and girls) to make a wedding related decision by themselves. If they are too young or naïve—they may be blindly attracted to each other. Every now and then we hear news of a young couple in love committing suicide, either alone or together, when their parents are unwilling to let them marry. Certainly, those young girls and boys do not have mature minds. They are influenced by love stories in the movies or suffering from blind attraction towards each other which is natural.

These days boys and girls are also getting into other kind of relations because they spend more time with each other. The kind where they get into a relationship after much deliberation. They plan for their future lives. They get married. Young people forming relationships like this are more mature. Now "career weddings" are taking place as well.

Our scriptures (Puran) describe the custom of *svayamvar* (*svayam* means self and *var* means husband), where a girl chooses her husband herself. There was never a custom of "*svayam-kanya*" (self-bride). Meaning, only the girls had the right to choose a life partner, not boys. Girls had a very strong basis for the selection of their life partners. They did not select life partners by getting swept away by emotion. They tried to find men whose qualities would match their own. They wanted husbands who were equipped with qualities to make their lives successful. Therefore, they chose husbands who were physically strong, intelligent, and experts in various skills.

Take Sita's *svayamvar* for example. I told you stories from the Ramcharitmanas (Lord Rama's story) in your childhood. You know that Sita, from a very young age, was able to lift the *Shiva-dhanush* (Shiva's bow) kept in her father King Janak's court. Her father took a vow that he would give Sita's hand in marriage to the young man who is able to lift that divine bow. Certainly, fathers used to wish for suitable husbands for their daughters. Similarly, in the Mahabharata, Draupadi's father Drupad took a vow that his daughter would marry the man who was able to hit an arrow into a fish's eye hanging above while looking at its reflection below in a bowl of oil. Now think. The boys had to go through such hard tests in those *svayamvars*! There used to be an intense competition among the boys to win a girl's hand in marriage. If they passed, they could be selected as grooms. Girls were also trained and educated accordingly. There was no field of life that girls were barred from entering.

Now that time has returned. Through hard work, girls have made a place for themselves in every field of life. Their eyes are wide open now. With open eyes, they are seeing the world and also their own future. In these circumstances, they have also gained the freedom to select life partners suitable for them. These type of arranged marriages are also taking place nowadays. Boys and girls are finding life partners after much thought and deliberation.

The perspective of parents has also changed with time. They have started to understand that when the boys and girls stay unmarried until 25-30 years of age, work together, get to know and understand each other—then they will likely choose their life partners amongst themselves. What is the harm in this? After all, they are the ones who need to spend their lives together. Let them choose their partners. Let them get married. But parents do plan their children's wedding in a traditional way for their own satisfaction, even while taking their children's decisions into account. Come on! They at least have this right. Children, too, like the Indian traditional weddings. They are truly special. I will expand on the traditions and customs of an Indian wedding another time.

Today I want to tell you only this—the traditional society that once used to believe in letting the youth select their life partners transformed and came to a point where it took away that freedom of choice from them. Parents became the decision makers. They would not consult with their children in their wedding related matters. Innumerable such marriages have even been successful. Today many of the young men and women who are trying to select their life partners after thoughtful consideration keep on thinking for a long time. Even after a long relationship, they decide to go separate ways. They do not like each other's company after having children. They are not able to make the decision to stay together. It is an experimental world after all. Scientific! Experiments are being done even in marriages—an important decision of personal life. And in this process, many lives are lived without marriage.

Marriage proposals for your elder brother Nawin had started coming. We were discussing those proposals. One day, one of his friends asked him, "*Yaar* (friend), have you seen the girl? Did you share your thoughts with your parents?"

We heard Nawin respond, "*Yaar*, these things are for the parents to take care of. They are experienced in this field. Let them think carefully and make the decision. Why should we interfere?" This is also one of the perspectives the youth have.

According to our *shastras* (scriptures), eight types of marriages are acceptable in society. Therefore, the changes taking place now in the decision-making and forms of marriages are not new to our society. In fact, the main goal of a marriage is to sustain, move forward, and stay durable. It is not important who makes the decision. Even if you decide yourself, there should not be a long delay. It should not come to a stage where you are only thinking about marriage. Whether it is a love-marriage or an arranged-marriage, determined by parents or by orthodox priests, intra-caste or inter-caste, national or international—the only thing that matters is the durability of the marriage. While the breaking of a marriage is hurtful for both parties, its lifelong durability is a source of joy for many.

I am wandering off topic again. Now you will say, "Mom, please stop now." Alright, I will stop. But I do want to know if you have thought further about that friend of yours or is he still in the "friend" category? Whatever it is, do write. Feel free to seek our help in making a decision. Many young people take a long time to tell their parents about their love interests. First, their selection process is long drawn out, and even after reaching a decision they take a long time before telling their parents. On the other hand, the parents start getting worried once the children are getting older. They start looking for marriage prospects. Sometimes they even give their word to a family. Then it becomes stressful for both sides.

It is possible to avoid this stress. Many young men from India decided to get married in America (where they were studying or working). They have another wedding in India on their parents' request. Just think! How stressful it must be. Let me tell you about an incident from our region. Two men from two different villages met at a fair. One of them said, "I wanted my daughter to marry your son. I regret that it did not happen." The next year they met again in a Rama temple. They were both very happy. It came out in the conversation that the first man had a four-month-old grandson. The second man was blessed with a month-old granddaughter. The second man said, "You wanted to become my *samadhi* (the relationship between the fathers of the bride and groom), right? Look, God has answered your prayers. You can have your grandson marry my granddaughter." Before them were the idols of Rama and Sita. They decided to name the granddaughter Sita and the grandson Rama. This is what happened. Even after Sita's grandfather passed away, Rama's grandfather remembered their promise and asked for Sita's hand in marriage for Rama. Yes, marriages like these also took place in our society. And they were successful too.

Where did I get lost and I am asking you to think about so many things! In fact, all I want to say is that everything should happen in a timely manner. According to the Hindu philosophy, the appropriate age to get married is twenty-five years or older. From twenty-five to fifty years is the phase of *grihastha-ashram* (a phase of life devoted to family and household), followed by *vaan-prastha* (forest-dweller; retired life) until the age of seventy-five and then *sanyaas-ashram* (life of renunciation) until the age of hundred. How well thought-out this system was. Appropriate categorization of a lifespan according to the needs of a person's body and mind. If there is too much disturbance in this four-phase system of a hundred year-life, then it can lead to problems.

Your Mother

□

Festivals

Dear daughter Mili,

Blessings!

Vijayadashami. The tenth day of the *Shukla paksha* (waxing phase of the moon) in *Ashwin* month. Today is Dussehra (festival that marks the victory of Lord Rama over the demon king Ravana). Parents miss their children more during the festive season. We are feeling your absence and your brother's.

These last nine days, while some parts of the country have been performing prayer ceremonies for Goddess Durga, other parts have Ramleela (story of Rama in a play or musical format) performances going on, and yet other places have *garba* dance gatherings (communal dance that honors Goddess Durga) every evening. During the monsoon season, some areas were facing drought while others were dealing with horrible floods. There was chaos everywhere. Thousands of people become homeless in this season. Hundreds of people die due to lack of food or by drowning in the flood waters. The month of *Ashwin* creeps in quietly. In the *Krishna paksha* (waning phase of the moon), people perform *pitru tarpan*—a ritual where water is offered to the deceased ancestors. The purpose is to pay homage to your past seven generations. From the first day of the *Shukla paksha*, a festive mood spreads in the entire country with flavors that are somewhat similar or a little different across the various states. People start cleaning and refreshing their homes. Immersing themselves in Goddess Durga's worship or watching and listening to Lord Rama's life stories performed in every neighborhood, people forget their woes, their poverty. On seeing the thousands of decorative tents that are set up across the country for the Goddess's worship and for Ramleela, who can say that our country is poor? Millions of rupees are spent every year. A man who can only afford to eat two *rotis* (flatbread) a day—even he takes out a coin from his torn shirt pocket and offers it to the Goddess. His one-rupee coin, fallen in the feet of the Goddess, is no less valuable that the various gems, pearls, and gold ornaments that the Goddess is decked up in.

I have always felt while observing people celebrating the various festivals and traditions that occur every month according to the weather— "Without these festivals, how would people who do not have clothes, food, or shelter in India stay alive?" Although, in our country, there are instances of several generations of a family continuing to live in poverty. Our ancestors have weaved thousands of short-long stories into the society's midframe, by way of which even the poorest person is filled with a determination to live life, a hope that the days will improve. Stories have been written to reduce the arrogance of the people sitting at the peak of power and wealth. Festivals and traditions have been created with that goal.

Utsav (festival) means to rise above.

In North India, Ramleela is performed on the stage in ten parts over the ten days of the Dussehra festival. Even the simplest man is shown Ramleela and made to understand the significance of Rama's life. The victory of good over evil. Every year on the day of Dussehra, thousands of effigies of Ravana (the evil king in Rama's story) are burnt all over the country. Vijaydashami (or Dussehra) is the day of Rama's coronation as king of Ayodhya. Weapons of all sorts are worshipped on this day in every household. There are processions of all sizes.

How can I not miss you in these times? We made some

delicacies at home too. When I cook something special, I miss you a lot. I wonder what you might have eaten. My mother-in-law used to invariably become sad on days of festivities. All her children had left home. Whenever she found me scolding my little kids, she used to say sadly, "Do not get upset. They will all fly away one day. Your nest will get empty. You will be sitting alone like me." I did not understand her words at that time. I was in a hurry in those days—when will my kids grow up, when will they be independent? Now I miss my mother-in-law a lot. You and your brother have gone so far away. Now I wish my kids had stayed little. This is the fate of human life. We are never content in the state we are in.

On the nine days of Goddess worship, I have prayed for the well-being of all of you. I only ask for peace of mind when I bow in front of the Goddess. That is plenty. God gives courage. Courage to endure pain. Courage to control the mind in happiness. That is why, in order to be successful, it is important to pray for a strong mind. Always keep a small idol of Goddess Durga with you. Before going to bed, say a few lines of *Durga Saptashati* (prayer). You must put in the effort (*karma*). It is important to make a resolution in order to reach your goal. Resolutions help control the mind. When we pray to God, our resolve becomes stronger. That is all. It is not that God will answer your prayers by studying your books for you. But by dedicating oneself to God, one becomes more interested in attaining one's goals. It helps speed up the work.

Twenty-five years ago, when you were only two months old, a twenty-five-years-old woman had asked me, "Aunty, why does my mother force me to go to the temple to pray? God is everywhere. Whenever I get a chance during the day, I can remember God. Why it is important to go to the temple or the *puja ghar* (many Hindu homes have prayer room or a dedicated area where God(s) is enshrined) to remember God?"

I said to her, "Look, an educated mother can teach her own child. Then why send them to school? It is because if she wants to teach the child at home, she may not be able to teach every day and every subject because she has many responsibilities in the house. Even if she teaches five hours every day, she may not be able to teach math, English, Hindi, and science. In school, there are specific periods for all subjects. Hindi will be taught during the Hindi period, and English in the English period. So, in the school, a child learns all subjects every day. In the same way, if you do not specify a time and place to remember God, you will never do it. That is why we go to pray in a temple or in our prayer rooms."

That young woman liked what I said. I do not know if she started going to the temple, but she certainly did not raise this question in front of me again.

I am wandering off topic again. If you were here, you would have said, "Mom, where do you get lost? You have become used to giving speeches."

You are right! There I was—missing you while making delicacies in the kitchen, and how far I have gone from there. This is not a lecture. If you lived in India, you would be able to celebrate, rejoice, and become a part of the festivities and the rituals. After leaving one's society, people still celebrate their traditions, but the traditions are not able to take the form of festivals.

Your Mom

□

Meeting and Parting

Dear Mili,

Have a long life!

I went to Suriname (South America) to participate in the Seventh World Hindi Conference. Suriname is a small country in South America. Population of only 500,000. More than 400 Hindi lovers and volunteers had come to participate from India and other countries. Before leaving, a thought crossed my mind, "Why go to Suriname? Why go to a small country to talk about Hindi? How much will that help with the development of Hindi?"

But after reaching there, my thinking changed. It was also important to visit that country to see how the Indians living there, in a very different environment, had kept the language, Indian-ness, and our traditions alive. Laborers were taken from India to Suriname 130 years ago. They endured very painful lives there. Now their fourth generation is living there. They are educated and wealthy, and even hold high political positions. I was very happy to see and hear this. We were staying at the Torarika Hotel in Suriname's capital city, Paramaribo. I went for a morning walk with Dr. Aruna Sitesh. Within a short distance, we came across mango trees. The trees were laden with fruit. My heart was thrilled when I saw the fruit-laden trees in the distance. When we came closer, I saw some mangoes fallen on the ground. Excitedly, I started picking up some mangoes. Dr. Aruna was a little hesitant.

Then she too joined me in picking up the mangoes. We were delighted holding five small mangoes each in our hands. We returned to the hotel in a very happy mood. We knocked on Chitra Mudgalji's door and as soon as she opened the door, we handed her all the mangoes. I said, "Today your day will be spent in joy. Look, you got mangoes as soon as you opened your eyes. And we will be joyful too, because we had the pleasure of gifting fruit first thing in the morning."

Truly, we were happy the whole day. Two months ago, I was in Patna's Circuit House (a guest house for government employees). After dinner, I was taking a stroll with Dr. Taaran Roy. In the Circuit House compound, small bunches of mangoes were looking beautiful hanging from the branches of mango trees. One small mango fell on my head. I was overjoyed. I asked, "Taaran, tell me something. Why does it make the heart so happy to see a fruit-laden tree, a field full of crop, a river full of water, and a mother feeding her baby?"

Taaran was silent. She was thinking. I said, "Look. I have found an answer to this 'why'. I have been traveling all over India for the past twenty years. When I travel by train or car, there is a strange sort of happiness I feel when I see fields full of crops, first green and then becoming golden. One day a question arose in my mind—all these years why did these sights bring me joy? Thinking about it, I found the answer and that is—inside every human being is a vast soul that finds joy in seeing others satiated. No one person or one family is going to eat so much fruit or so much grain by themselves. But when the crop is good, every wise mouth is heard saying, 'This year has been joyful. The crop is very good.' The feeling is that many people will be fed by the crop. No one will stay hungry. Finding joy in feeding others is indeed a sign of being human. This is being motherly. Being equitable. And this motherliness is in all of us in some measure, in both men and women. Feeling satiated after making someone else's stomach full. And this is why it brings us joy to see a fruit-laden tree, a full river, and a full field. The feeling is akin to feeling full without having eaten anything. The state of being full shows completeness—of the tree, the river, and the fields. It shows their nature as well as their destiny."

It was the month of June and in Suriname it was the season of mangoes, jackfruit, and many other fruits. I was delighted by seeing the fruits on the trees. And then I met Durga *behen* (sister). Durga Udit Dube (whose family was from India) took me in her car to her house for a little while. I was in a hurry, so I told her I would not enter the house. Standing in her yard, she kept saying (in Bhojpuri), "What should I give you? I must give something to my sister who has come to my house from the land of my *nani-dadi* (maternal and paternal grandmothers). Then she plucked two *amra* fruits (hog plum) from a tree in her yard and gave them to me. I said, "We also have this tree in my village. We make chutneys and pickles with *amra*. But here the *amra* fruit is very big in size. The tree is very small. In fact, it is more like a bush, not a tree."

Then she gave me some curry leaves from a tree that was in the neighbor's yard that had barbed fencing. The leaves smelled wonderful. She quickly broke several stems and gave them to me. Now think—why would I take those two things back to India when they are grown here too? But I had to because they were from Durga's yard after all. She had plucked them for me very lovingly. I brought those two small *amra* fruits and the stems of curry leaves back to India.

I am reminded of an episode from several years ago. I was living in Delhi with you and your brothers. Your father and his younger brother Abhay Singh lived in our house in Muzaffarpur (Bihar). I took you along with me when I went to visit him every second or third month. One time I went around January-February. Seeds were being sown for vegetables that grow in the month of *Baisakh* (April-May). We used to grow many vegetables in our yard in that house. I put in seeds of bitter gourd, bottle gourd, cucumber, and many other vegetables. Your father was coming to Delhi in the month of April. We had become used to bringing *paraval* (pointed gourd) and other vegetables from Muzaffarpur to Delhi. He bought many vegetables from the market. And among the five kilos of *paraval* and plantain, there were also two small bitter gourd, two little okra, and one cucumber. Our helper burst out laughing while taking the vegetables out of the tote bag. He thought, "The vegetable vendor must have put these in the bag by mistake." But I understood immediately. The seeds I had sown in January-February could only have produced these tiny vegetables by April. Your Abhay *chacha* (uncle) had sent them for me. He thought of me to this extent. That was not a small thing. He knew that his loving gesture was light in weight but heavy in emotion. It would reach deep in my heart and make a permanent place for itself. And that is what happened. I have not forgotten that episode to this date. Occasionally, I remember and immerse myself in the emotion sent by him.

A person gets attached to some, gets separated from others. This attachment and separation is called life. I found the people of Suriname to be big-hearted. They have kept the traditions from their villages alive over the last three-four generations. This is not a simple thing. Everything is changing now in the Indian city life. One gentleman from Suriname was sharing his thoughts during a session in the conference, and said, "When I met Dr. Vidyanivas Mishra (a renowned expert of Hindi in India) in 1985, I told him that we are keeping the Indian traditions alive in Suriname, but India is changing a lot. He replied, 'You people keep the traditions alive. After everything dies here, it will return to India again from your country.' We are trying to keep the tradition going even in our fourth generation—language, food, festivals and rituals, worship rituals, and everything."

I brought Durga along to my hotel room. We had met only three hours ago. It felt as if we had known each other for a long time. We had become intimate despite knowing that it was our first and perhaps our last meeting. She was saying again and again (in Bhojpuri), "*Didi* (elder sister), I am glad I met you, but it was for too short a time."

With her saying this repeatedly, I could feel that she had found my company pleasant, and I hers. She kept telling me about her three sons and one daughter. She said, "We do not have a lot of money. But I am satisfied. I do not wish for more."

She kept asking me about my family. She referred to her husband as *Pundit* (priest). We met for dinner again the same evening. She said to me, "*Didi,* my *Pundit* was tired. He had gone to help with a funeral during the day." She kept talking about her husband in a motherly way. In talking with her, it did not feel at all that she was from a different society. She sang one *bhajan* (dev) that evening. That *bhajan* is sung in our region too. She told me she goes to sing *bhajans* at the Durga temple.

In front of Hindu homes, I saw flags hoisted on bamboo sticks. Several bamboo sticks were tied together. I was reminded of my village. We left our culture in the villages when we moved to the cities. These people had kept everything alive for more than 150 years. Salute to them!

Despite being so close to your Cornell University (New York), I have returned to India without seeing you. There were several reasons. You (and your brother and sister-in-law) are so busy in your work. I too have a lot of work in my country. Everyone is busy—whether it is a child, youth, or the elderly. Even after retirement, people start looking for new work. Work has taken over our lives. There should be some time for leisure too.

Even in Suriname, I was curious to learn about nature. We kept talking with them to enjoy hearing stories related to their attempts to grow herbs using seeds taken from India. That was a long way to travel—yet we do not even have the time to enjoy the fruit and flower-laden trees and shrubs we planted around us in India. We are so busy in our work, which creates more boredom than enjoyment.

I am reminded of several incidents from even before you were born. We had bought land to build a house in Muzaffarpur. Construction began on the house. The plot was big. I was also in a hurry to start growing vegetables. I planted a few eggplant plants in one corner. The soil was not tilled properly, so the roots of the eggplant saplings were very thin. Yet, the saplings started flowering. We used to go visit the site every morning and evening. While your father would discuss construction work with the workers, I would go check on the eggplant. In some time, a little fruit emerged. That morning, while looking at the fruit I said, "I will pluck it tomorrow and feed it to my younger son (who was one year old)." That very evening your father went to the site again. When he returned, he said to me, "There is one sad news for you." I inquired instantly, "Did the goat eat the eggplant?"

He said, "yes," and started assessing the depth of the pain that had spread over my face. In fact, that morning I had seen the neighbor's goat that was tied up nearby. I even told one of the construction workers, "Ask the goat owner to take it away." Certainly, that man did not understand the importance of that tiny eggplant for me. But for me it was not just a tiny eggplant. It was the first fruit grown on our land, and on top of that, I had wanted to feed that to our young son. That small two-inch eggplant had made so many ties with my heart. There are many such incidents from my life that are associated with fruits and vegetables. They bring joy. It was 1974, before you were born. We had returned from Patna to Muzaffarpur after four days. It was the month of April. It was getting dark. There were many visitors on the front patio. While we were talking with them, it became darker. After seeing them off, we should have gone inside the house. We had left our young sons with their *Dadi* (paternal grandmother), and we had not seen them for four days. But we took a flashlight and went straight to our vegetable patch. We were thrilled to see the little new vegetables that had come up. Little bitter gourd and bottle gourd, etc., glowing happily in our torch light.

Life is about staying connected with nature. That life brings pleasure. The farther we go from nature, the more we start searching for happiness. But we are not finding joy in this search. Planting crops, vegetables, or trees fills us with hope, and we feel joyful when that hope is fulfilled. Then a new hope rises for the new crop.

These days, people are growing jungles in the cities with multi-story apartments. When I see these concrete jungles deprived of trees, this thought rises in my mind, "How will the people living here find joy?" I say to the residents there, "You should plant trees as soon as possible. And if possible, plant fruit trees. They will provide shade as well as fruit." As one saying goes, "Trees are like our ancestors. Their shade cools even a burning body."

I saw many other things in Suriname. I will keep telling you about them now and then. To inspire you to keep your culture and traditions alive even while living in America, just like the Suriname-people have. If you need to live there, then live, but also set up your village around you. Just like the people in Suriname, Fiji, Guyana, and Mauritius have done.

There is only one difference between you and them. They were taken to those countries as laborers. That is why they kept their Ramcharitmanas alive. Educated Indians are now going to America and England. Those people had already shed many aspects of the Indian culture even while living in India. They did not take the Geeta and the Ramayana with them.

While raising you in Delhi, I tried to keep our village alive in you. You have preserved it too. I am very happy about that.

Blessings!
Your Mom

□

The Joy of Living in a Hermitage

Dear daughter Mili,

Blessings!

Good, now you are relieved of this one worry. Your student life of twenty-five years has come to an end. This is a difficult phase of life, but also enjoyable. A golden time for opportunities in human life. It was an experience for you to travel to different cities in America for job interviews. You had that opportunity. And now you have the job. I know that these days you must be preparing to establish yourself in your new role. I am confident that, as always, you will make a special place for yourself in this new job. Dear, it is a very special quality to be sincere towards your work. A person who handles small responsibilities earnestly in his childhood also completes all his responsibilities when he grows up. Managing responsibilities is not a problem for him, and neither does he have to work too hard. He becomes accustomed to it.

These days I am in an *ashram* (hermitage)—the Panchdas Alakhwara Ashram established in Rikhiya village in the Devghar district of Jharkhand state. It is a branch of Yogbharati which is in Munger. My knees hurt. I came here to learn yoga to treat the pain. I did not know then that coming here will cleanse not only my body, but also my mind. These days Navratri is being observed. Ramacharitamanas (the story of Lord Rama) is divided into nine parts and each part is recited over the nine days of Navratri. During this time, Nav Durga is also recited. Every year in this *ashram,* this Navratri program is conducted twice a year in Ashwin and Chaitra months. Young boys and girls who are getting an education here are the ones who recite the Ramacharitamanas and the Durga Saptashati. We recite along with them.

In the large meeting hall of the *ashram,* it is very pleasing to hear almost one thousand people reciting the *R*amacharitamanas in unison every day for three hours. There is no difference here between the young and the elderly. The tiers made in the society on the basis of religion, caste, and wealth have ended here. This *ashram's Swami* Niranjandevji and *Swamini* Santsangiji are also having meals with us and doing the daily recitations with us. Three hundred people have lunch and dinner (as early as 5:00 pm) together every day.

When there is an event in the family, we get exhausted providing meals for 20-25 people for two days. In this place, everything is happening very smoothly. You do not have to raise your voice to ask for anything to be done. There are no appointed helpers here. The devotees are eager to help, and they are doing everything from sweeping the floors to doing yard work, cleaning the bathrooms, chopping vegetables, and serving *rotis* (flatbread). Even little children are involved in doing all the chores. Three generations are mingling. *Dada-dadi* (grandparents) are doing physical labor alongside *pota-poti* (grandchildren).

In the eight days since I have been here, I have not read a newspaper or watched television, have not slept under an electric fan—but I am not missing those things.

The appearance and function of the meeting hall changes five times every day. The *ashram* wakes up at 3:00 am. By 5:00 am everyone is ready and gathers in the meeting hall. Yoga is taught. The breakfast bell rings at 6:00 am. The meeting hall is then decorated and ready by 8:00 am. All the devotees gather for a recitation of the Ramcharitmanas. The recitation lasts for three hours without any rest or interruption. The harmonious sound of the recitation is very beautiful and pleasing. The little girls participating have practiced so much. Sister Mantranidhiji, who has come from Munger with specialized training, starts the recitation. There are distinct tunes set for singing every couplet, metre, and quatrain of the Ramcharitmanas. Everyone sings in those specific tunes.

I am remembering your childhood. A little girl, Nirupama, around four years old has come here from Delhi with her parents and brother. That little girl is a main center of attraction in the *ashram* these days. Everyone feels happy seeing her. They talk to her. She participates in all the activities in the *ashram.* She claps excitedly while reciting Durga-stuti (prayers for Goddess Durga). She dances all around us while singing the *bhajans* with us. She is not shy at all in a crowd of a thousand people. She also knows many *shlokas* and *mantras* (Hindu chants) by heart. When I see her, I see you. You were just like she is. You were also used to being in crowds of a thousand or two thousand people. In a big gathering like that, you were never shy to accompany me on the stage. On the contrary, you used to nag at me if I chose to not be seated on the main stage.

Now I think that those small opportunities that came in your life were not unimportant. They filled you with self-confidence from a very young age. Partly because of your natural abilities and partly because of your surroundings, you were able to recite lines from the Ramcharitmanas at the age of four. You knew by heart couplets and quatrains by Rahiman, Kabir, and Tulsi. By the time you were four years, you had also learnt to read and write Hindi. This was not an ordinary thing. I used to keep teaching you while running errands. Even while traveling on a rickshaw, car, or train, I used to make you memorize couplets. One day you were reciting lines from the Ramcharitmanas, *"Bhaye Pragat Kripala, Deen Dayala...."* On seeing you, Kailashpati Mishraji, who was very fond of you, was amazed. You used to accompany me on trips from a very young age. And in some time, you became an expert in traveling. What precautions to take during travel, what to pack—you knew everything. Sometimes you would remind me too.

Environment plays an important role in children's development. Children who live in the surrounding areas of this *ashram* are very lucky. They are so close to this *ashram*. They have learnt a lot. The little girls who recite the Ramayana for three hours every day here barely knew how to sit and stand properly three years ago when they were asked to come here. They have memorized many chapters from the Geeta. Children are certainly getting a good education in big cities like Delhi and Mumbai, but that education is only good to fill the stomach (earn a living). The education imparted by the *ashram* is for the development of body, mind, intellect, as well as the soul. I am delighted to see the good luck of these children. Many seeds of personality development have been sown in them.

My heart is pleased for another reason. Here the young girls and women have a more dominant role. Historically, there was no discrimination between sons and daughters in our society. Daughters also studied the Vedas (ancient scriptures). They wrote the *mantras* for the Vedas. Mandan Mishra's wife Bharati had an intellectual debate with Shankaracharya. She won the debate against Shankaracharya. There are many episodes like these. But in the middle-ages, the development of women was gradually blocked. An incorrect belief spread in the society that women are not equal to men in the Hindu religion. Indian families started becoming male dominant. Now again, social and religious institutions are giving equal opportunities to girls in fields that were considered exclusive for boys. Today, with encouragement from the society, girls are placing their feet firmly on land, water, and sky. Girls are progressing in every field of life. It is said that *ashram* life is a reflection of the modern Indian way of life. It is a matter of joy that in every field of life, a return to Indian-ness has begun.

I found one more special thing about this *ashram*. It does not only foster a person's spiritual development. The institution operates with the goal of an all-round development of each person. A healthy soul can develop only in a healthy body.

I came here because of my knee pain. The camp was for twenty days. I did learn many yoga techniques, but also got the opportunity to see and learn many other things. All the people staying (temporarily) at the *ashram* used to start doing *seva* (service) first thing in the morning. No one asked anyone to work. Everyone was working of their own will, so everything seemed smooth and easy. The whole environment was very pleasant.

Food was simple, but delicious. No one had any complaints with the food. Nirupama, too, used to sit with everyone and sip her tea in a small earthen cup. Wisdom to live life was not being taught in theory. Each theory was being put into practice. Nirupama is a lucky girl. You too had the opportunity to live in camps when you were as old as her.

The day I came here, I was worried how ten days would pass. Now while leaving it feels as if ten days were over in a few minutes. In just a few days, I have made connections with many people. The thought of separation makes me sad. People of the *ashram* are requesting that I visit again. A quatrain by Tulsidasji has come alive while bidding farewell to them—there are some people meeting whom causes much pain, and then there are some parting from whom is like losing one's life. It is true, parting from good people is not easy. Whether they are from your country or not.

I will call you back to India around this time next year. You too should spend ten days in that *ashram*. You will find it joyful. It will bring a new light to your life.

In fact, *ashram* life has had a particular importance in

India. Students used to go stay in their *guru's ashram* to get an education. There have been *ashrams* for the elderly too.

The special quality of this *ashram* was that people of all ages—from a four-year-old girl to an eighty-year-old elderly man—stayed there together.

With best wishes,
Your Mom

□

Partners in Success

Dear Mili,

Live a long life!

The telephone rang. I picked up the receiver. You had called just an hour ago. Before leaving for your thesis defense, you had called for our blessings—which are always with you. Your father and I had given you our best wishes. As usual you were nervous. You had not been able to sleep all night. But we were confident that you would be successful. Even after putting in an honest effort for every exam, you have always been doubtful about the results. And we along with you. Because our bodies may be separate, but our hearts are not.

Yes, so the voice on the phone said, "This is Dr. Sinha speaking." The voice was indeed yours. But it took a few minutes to internalize it, because I had thought your thesis defense would last longer. We were surprised when you called within an hour and declared yourself a doctor. I congratulated you. And gave many blessings. You asked, "Is Dr. Sinha home?" You were asking about your brother Dr. Praveen Sinha. His support has also been important for your success. I said, "He has left for work. You can call him on his cell phone." You asked, "Is Senior Dr. Sinha at home?" I handed the phone receiver to your father. Tears started rolling down my face. They were tears of joy. Your accomplishment, my success. I called several of our relatives to tell them the news. In India, your elder brother Nawin and *Bhabhi* (sister-in-law) Sangita were very happy, of course. Other relatives were also happy to hear the news.

We were in Madison, Wisconsin, at your brother's place. We had gone to attend your Ph.D. convocation ceremony. Six of us (including your two small nephews) left for Ithaca, New York. Praveen had made your five-year-old nephew Dhruv learn this line, "My *bua* (father's sister) has become a doctor."

It was a joyful time. We reached Cornell University. You were busy preparing for your convocation ceremony. But you were also making arrangements for our stay and meals whole-heartedly. On the first day, Cornell University's 137th convocation ceremony took place in the big Barton Hall on campus. Five Hundred students from your department, from undergraduates to PhDs, had to walk up to the podium to collect their degrees. We chose to sit in a place from where we could clearly see you walk up on the podium. After all, that was the only purpose of us flying across the seven seas. You were fourth in the line of students to enter the hall. The PhDs in the front of the line were wearing robes and hoods in a different color from the other students. Our eyes teared up again seeing you in your robe with its special color. I was overwhelmed with emotion seeing you enter the hall from the back door and walk in line towards the stage. The hall was echoing with nonstop applause. Your Praveen *bhaiya* (elder brother) was running from one corner of the hall to another trying to take your pictures. No sign of tiredness. His heart was happy, so the body had a lot of energy. In fact, he considers your success to be his own success. Your school and college friends from India, Anuja Jayaraman and Sushil Kumar, had also come from other states to attend the ceremony. Only to see you in your special robe.

The next day, four thousand graduating students at the university were going to march from a fixed place to the football stadium. We reached the stadium at nine in the morning. It was a festive environment. Crowds of men, women, and children were entering the stadium. There were several entrances, all crowded. But there was no chaos, no panic. In just a short while, fifty thousand people filled the stands of the stadium. The graduating students were about to parade into the stadium. We were seated very far. students receiving their PhDs were first to enter the stadium. It was hard to recognize you from a distance as all the students were in the same gown. Then we found you. Our eyes teared up again. The weather forecast said rain, but the skies were clear. The spring sun was shining in the month of May. Grandparents, parents, friends, and relatives of four thousand graduating students were seated in the stands. They were making cheering sounds again and again.

Seated next to me was a student's grandmother, her eyes pouring, making the weather prediction accurate. The president of Cornell University congratulated the parents and grandparents too at the start of his speech. It was a celebration of success of the students' effort. Certainly, the mothers and fathers were also contributors in their success.

But the accomplishment was the students' indeed. You had no time to breathe. You have been studying for the last twenty-five years. Finally, your education is complete. You are relieved. One out of the four phases of life is now over for you. The *bramhacharya ashram* (student phase) is now complete. In this phase, you learnt the art of living life. This is the foundation for the rest of your life.

In the late stages of life (*vanaprastha ashram*; life of renunciation), people find joy in their children's accomplishments. Every little thing you did as a child used to bring us joy. It has been joyful just to look at you. Your leaving India and going across the seven seas was certainly painful, or I should say it was a bittersweet experience. One night you had called when it was 3:00 in the morning in India. You cried on the phone, "Mom, I don't want to stay here. I am coming back to India." I said, "Yes, yes, come." Then you called again after some time, "Mom, I am alright."

Five years ago, I had come to Cornell University. When I

saw you living alone, I had felt that I would definitely not be able to live there if I had to. But how could I say that to you? You were already there, so you had to finish your studies. How could I discourage you? But when are parents ever at peace after sending their children off to another country? On festivals and holidays, we missed you a lot. You would always ask on the phone, "Mom, what did you eat?" I would lie, "Not much. One *sabzi* (vegetables), *daal* (lentils), and *roti-chawal* (flatbread and rice)." When, in fact, there would be many delicacies cooked at home. Once, on the day of Holi (festival of color), you had asked, "Mom, what did you cook today?" I said, "Not much." You replied, "Mom, why do you hide things from me? *Pua* (fried pancakes), *kheer* (rice pudding), *chhole* (chickpeas), *kathal ke vade* (jackfruit fritters), *poori* (fried bread), and so much more you used to cook on Holi. I am sure you have made these."

And then you said, "I too have cooked all these things that you used to cook on Holi. I will invite my friends and serve it to them." I was satisfied. Then I told you that your *Bhabhi* (sister-in-law) had made many things too.

If it was up to the parents, they would never let their children go far away. But they have to for the sake of their children's future. If the children get a good education, good *sanskaar* (values), a good job, then parents feel happy. When I was eight years old (in 1950), my father had sent me to a boarding school. When my matriculation exam results came out (in 1958), my father said, "Today I am the happiest person in the world." My mother had asked, "Only you, not me?"

On seeing you march confidently in your graduation robe in that football stadium, I felt as if I was the happiest person in the world. Seated next to me, your father's eyes were tearing up now and again. After matriculation, I continued my education to receive a master's degree, then taught in a college as a lecturer, and then became the founder-Principal of an elementary school. There was only one goal behind the honest effort I put into all these roles—to make my father happy. What is wrong with having a life goal of making others happy—your parents, your siblings, or your educators? Many good things are accomplished even with this goal. You often say, "Nawin *bhaiya* asked me to do a Master's in Economics, so I did it. Praveen *bhaiya* asked me to do a PhD in Finance, so I did it. When did I make a decision for myself?"

The degrees you received are yours. Your efforts kept bearing fruit. But those family members were also pleased who made you a medium to fulfil their hopes.

Old age is certainly spent in a more relaxing and happy manner when your children turn out to be good. Wealth is definitely important to find happiness in life, but wealth is not everything. Wealth is a medium, not a goal. You have accepted a good job offer in America. You will earn in dollars. Sitting far away in India, your parents, your brother and sister-in-law, nieces, along with other relatives and friends from childhood to youth—they will rejoice in your accomplishments, and this should be a matter of joy for you.

I had the opportunity to meet several young Indian men and women during this visit to America. It made me happy to learn that they care for their parents' feelings despite being so far away. They think about their parents' joys and sorrows. They want to bring them happiness by way of their accomplishments. This is what all parents expect from their children. When these expectations are not met by the children, then old age feels like a burden.

We are very lucky that our three children, two daughters-in-law, and four grandchildren give us a lot of respect. Living with us is not burdensome for them. Academic degrees also have the purpose of making life happy and smooth. Even for you, your graduation day would perhaps not have been as festive if your father and I, your brother and sister-in-law, your nephews and your friends were not present. And we would certainly have been deprived of a very big joy if we had not taken part in the ceremony. Several of your friends who were graduating said to me, "Aunty, I wish my mom and dad were here too. They would have really loved it." Their parents were not able to leave India for some reason.

Many blessings to you. You will continue bringing us joy. Because it becomes a lifelong habit to feel happy by making others happy. It is an addiction. When one gets addicted to this, then that's it. Your life becomes joyful. You had fallen prey to this addiction from a very young age.

With wishes for a life full of happiness,
Your Mom

□

Farewell Message

My daughter Mili,

Blessings!

Your Kamod *mama*'s (maternal uncle) daughter Julie got married. I am sending you the letter that was sent to her by her mother. Hope you will share it with your friends (non-Indians too).

My blessed daughter,

May your marriage last forever!

With your wedding ceremony completed, you are now connected with two families. Now, acting as a bridge between the two families, you must make them both flourish. This is why you will be called a *duhita* (one who benefits two families). Each of the rituals that were a part of Varun and your Hindu wedding ceremony has a special meaning. All the rites and rituals express the deep significance of a married life. Out of the sixteen Hindu rituals, the wedding ritual is of greatest importance. From a spiritual point of view, a wedding is the ideal unification of humans and nature. It is not just for the worldly life. This is why in our culture a marriage is considered to be a relationship spanning many lives.

Your wedding ceremony had three parts—*kanya-daan* (gift of a daughter), *laja-hom* (offering of puffed rice to the sacred fire), and *sapta-padi* (seven steps). Each ritual has its own significance. You should reflect on the deep import of these rituals over the course of your life. *Kanya-daan* was a ceremony involving your parents (us), *laja-hom* involved your brother, and *sapta-padi* was about you. We felt as if we (your father and I) were the proposers of your wedding, your brother and other relatives were approvers, and you yourself were a supporter of this ceremony by performing the *sapta-padi* ritual. Members of Varun's and your families were witnesses.

While reciting the Ved *mantras,* leaving our family and joining your husband's family forever, in the form of a daughter-in-law—you have prayed to never get separated from that family. The meaning of marriage is—having lawfully earned each-other, to carry on your mutual responsibilities. But even in this ceremony, the main role was yours. So you will have the special responsibility to carry it on.

Your father performed an invocation of the Gods and prayed for your husband Varun's long life. He dedicated you to the other family as an extension of his soul. He seated Varun in the wedding pavilion in the form of God Narayan. Very respectfully, he said to Varun, "Lord Narayan, you have blessed our house with your presence. My daughter, a form of Goddess Laxmi, is now your precious belonging. I offer her in the care of your pristine hands. Please accept her."

Varun, while touching his head respectfully to the offering of flowers, fruit, rice, and clothes, has made a promise to your father that he will always respect Goddess Laxmi in your human form. During the *pani-grahan* (hand-holding of bride and groom) ceremony, you were seated with us. Varun stood up, bowed, and asked to hold your hands. You were treated very respectfully. By saying the words "*amohamasmi*" you two have declared publicly, "We are performing this ceremony with full knowledge and deliberation."

During the *shila-rohan* ceremony, your brother assisted you with placing your foot on a small rock. Standing firm on the rock is symbolic—it implies that while handling your responsibilities as a wife and daughter-in-law, you will not tremble in the face of the biggest difficulties. And the assistance of your brother in this ceremony symbolizes that he will help you during hardships even after sending you off to your in-law's house.

With the assistance of your brother, you completed the *laja-hom* ritual using *shami-patra* (leaves of Ghaf tree) and *kheel* (puffed rice). *Shami* tree leaves stay green even in scorching heat. Always remember this message too that you should keep your behavior balanced like the *shami* tree whether you are facing extreme hardships or abundant fortunes.

The *kheel* (puffed rice) is representative of the galaxies glowing in the night sky. The galaxies shine during dark nights, not on moon-lit nights. My daughter, the *kheel* you used in the ritual taught you to live a balanced life. Stay humble in prosperity and brave in adversity.

In the *sapta-padi* ceremony, Varun and you walked around the holy fire seven times. The first time is for food, clothing, and shelter; the second is for strength; the third is for wealth and providing education to children; the fourth is for making decisions together; the fifth is for children; the sixth is for standing together in good and bad times; and the seventh is for lifelong companionship.

In the end, you made the groom accept your conditions. Your first condition was that he should never spend the night away from home unless it was required for a special reason. He should not even eat food outside. He promised.

Your second condition was, "Your happiness, sorrow, friends, family would all be mine; you would be my caretaker and fulfil all my needs." He agreed.

Your third condition was that you will strengthen yourself by adding his strength. He agreed.

The fourth thing you said was, "I will live for you. You will be concerned for me." He agreed.

Your fifth condition was, "Even when I get upset or fight with you, you would stay calm. You should not get upset." He agreed.

Your sixth condition was, "My parents raised me and did my *kanya-daan.* You will never remark on what gifts they have or have not given me." He agreed.

The seventh condition was that in all religious rites and rituals, you will be his partner. But you will not be his partner in any acts of sin. You also made him promise that you will not share your religious merits with him.

He also agreed to your condition that he will never have (physical) contact with another woman.

Then you stood up and sat on his left side. Your role was prominent in the wedding ceremony. If not for you, Varun and you could not have become a couple. Now he has started a family. My courtyard is blessed that a new married life is budding from here. After *sindoor-daan* (groom puts vermillion in bride's hair), you looked towards the North Star. You vowed to make your married life unfaltering like the North Star. Always remember that.

All the ceremonies related to the wedding kept making me happy. I stood by you as you took your vows. The night passed swiftly, and the sun rose. It was time to bid you farewell.

Today, you are leaving our house. As the time for your departure is coming closer, I am losing my composure. What is happening to me? I have never felt this way before in my life. This is the emotion that caused distress even to the stoic King Janak when he bid farewell to his daughter Sita.

We were in a rush to find a suitable groom for you for the last two years. When we fixed your match just two months ago, we felt very happy, as if we had reached a big milestone in life. Even while preparing for your wedding, we were excited. We were joyful. We had the desire to not leave anything lacking in your bridal attire. So, we went out of our budget to shop for you, to gather resources to welcome the groom party—and we did it all very enthusiastically. But when the groom's procession entered our courtyard and filled it with musical sounds from the band, our hearts felt a little jolt. There was a lot of work to be done. We did not have the time to hear our heartbeats. I could not afford to rest even for a moment. With every ritual of the wedding—*jayamala* (garland exchange), *kanya-daan, laja-hom, sapta-padi*—our hearts started beating faster. During the *laja-hom* and *sindoor-daan* ceremonies, it felt as if our hearts would tear apart. You left our family to sit with Varun's family. It felt like the lines from a folksong I had heard since childhood were becoming true, "If you were gold, daughter, I could have had you re-molded. Once you have *sindoor* (vermillion) in your hair (you are married), I cannot have you back."

You now belong to your groom after the *sindoor-daan* ceremony. I know that after going to his house, you will wilt for some time. But inside your heart there will be a joy, an excitement. You will bloom with Varun's love and respect. While bidding you farewell, I want to tell you a few things from experience as I place *jeera* (cumin seeds), *haldi* (turmeric), and *doob* (Durva grass) in the corner of your saree you are holding in your palms.

First, you are married to your groom, but your relationship is not just with him. The groom is someone's son, someone's brother, and has many other relationships. There is one easy way to have the groom be completely yours. The relationships he has been giving love and respect to, if you show even greater affection and respect for them as you make them your own, you will earn their respect as well as your husband's.

My dear daughter, your father was the ideal man for you so far. Feeling this way about your father was appropriate. But it is not necessary that your father is seated on the same high pedestal in your in-laws' eyes. You will have a big role to play in earning respect for your father in their hearts. So, for some time, keep the extreme respect you have for us hidden in your heart. Girls like everything about their parents' home. But it is not practical to keep singing praises of your parents' home all the time in your in-laws' house. Try to find good qualities in the people in your husband's family. This will be a beginning phase in your in-laws' house. Your situation will be akin to a paddy plant that is uprooted from one piece of land and transplanted in another. Everything is different—soil, air, water. I believe that in just a few days that house will start feeling like your own. On many occasions, you will not visit even if I invite you. After all, the problems of the new home will be yours too. But it will take some time for that stage to come. The stage of infancy is an important one. It is in this stage that seeds of *sanskaar* (culture; way of life) are sown, and qualities are cultivated. I am bracing myself. I will not ask about your in-laws' house too much. If you put the yogurt starter in the milk and keep stirring the milk, how will the yogurt set? I will not keep shaking a new sampling that has just been transplanted into a new wet soil. I will keep watering it. I will let your roots grow in your in-laws' house.

I could not keep you in our house forever. Make that other house your own as well. You will always have my support. This will bring me joy.

My blessed daughter, your mother-in-law has raised her son with a lot of love and dreams. She has sacrificed her happiness for him. The son raised by her will now be yours. Make sure you do not hurt her feelings at all. Make it so she can easily place your face right next to Varun's in her heart. This does not require any special effort. It would be best to keep your behavior natural.

I have complete confidence in you. Along with your studies, you gave your care and support to your grandparents, uncles, aunts, and me. You gave love to the younger ones. From observing you, I could tell that with these qualities you will find an appropriate place for yourself in your in-laws' house.

Daughter, there should not be any complaints from your in-laws'. Keep ignoring the small mistakes your husband makes. From a very young age, a woman has so much patience and courage that she tries to understand everyone's feelings and maintain her relationships. From now on, that will be your new home and you will be its foundation.

This advice is not meant to teach you to keep tolerating someone's criticism, torture, or disregard. It is possible to win anyone with a sweet voice, *seva* (service), and compassion.

The other three *ashrams* (phases of life) are dependent on *grihastha-ashram* (the married life), and the woman is the foundation of this phase. It is a huge responsibility on our shoulders! The greater the responsibility, the greater is the respect. To earn this respect, we must invest with serving our duty. The joy of serving your duty is special. And the taste of this joy increases further when each and every member of the (in-laws') family gives you authority.

There should not be a question of who among the two of you is superior—you or your husband. Keep in mind the *Ardha-nareeshwar* (God who is half-man, half-woman) form of Lord Shiva and Goddess Parvati.

Piece of my heart! The helpers of your new home are waiting for you eagerly. They will be delighted to have you there. They, too, will expect to be treated respectfully. Give them the appropriate emotion and treatment.

While bidding you farewell, I am placing a huge responsibility on your delicate shoulders. Until yesterday, you splashed in our eyes like a thin stream of tears, how will you expand to take the entire family in your embrace? Daughter, we believe that you will thrive in your new home, your personality will expand there.

Until now, you were a daughter here, a rightful owner of our love. You will now be an empress there. You will have authority.

Mother- and father-in-law, brother-in-law, sister-in-law, and helpers of the house—while ruling their hearts, how will our daughter find the time to care for us?

We have prayed to all the Gods-Goddesses and the entire world to ask for your *suhaag* (for one's husband to stay alive). I place an offering of blessings in your hands as I pray for the long life of your husband. I keep some *jeera* (cumin seeds) from the offering for myself. A woman's life is like that of Durva (*doob*) grass (one of the bridal farewell offerings). A patch of dry Durva grass, uprooted and thrown away, starts flourishing again when it finds soil. Keep flourishing, my daughter. Be your husband's lifelong companion, keep trying to make human life meaningful.

My darling, come, let me seat you in your *doli* (bridal carriage). I bid you farewell with an empty heart and tearful eyes. Look, everyone's eyes have teared up. These flowing streams of tears from our eyes will keep soaking and nurturing your new life, new role, and new responsibility.

Your Mother

Did you see? Your *mami* (maternal uncle's wife) said everything in this letter. She may not have been able to say all this verbally. She filled her daughter's *aanchal* (corner of a saree) with tips for a happy married life.

Your Mom

□

Symbols of Marriage

Dear daughter,

Blessings!

For these past few years, I have frequently had the opportunity to travel by Indian Airlines. Some months I have flown as many as ten or fifteen times on Indian Airlines flights. Sometimes, during the security check, the airport policewomen check me from head to toe using a security wand in their hand. And when they bend down to reach my feet with the wand, I automatically say "stay blessed" or "stay married forever." (In Hinduism, touching someone's feet is symbolic of paying respect and asking for blessings.)

Sometimes, the blessings I say out of habit reach the right place. Women in their khaki police uniform at the airports in Bihar, Orissa, Bengal, Uttar Pradesh, or Madhya Pradesh have a streak of vermillion (*sindoor*) in their hair parting. But in southern India or in the north, the women do not apply *sindoor.* You cannot even see if they are wearing a *mangal-sootra* (a necklace that symbolizes marriage) because their shirts are buttoned up all the way to the neck. Then how can I bless them to be a *suhagan* (woman whose husband is alive). In those situations, I have to say "*khush raho*" (stay happy). I know that for women, there is one blessing that is comparable to hundreds of "stay happy" blessings—"*sada suhagan raho*" (may your husband live forever). But this blessing only applies when the woman is married. In the name of modernism, many traditional conventions are being abandoned without any thought and consideration. One of them is the marriage symbol. In other words, there is no need to use marriage symbols to make a distinction between a woman who is married, unmarried, or a widow. Women felt the need to deny and erase the distinction based on different marital statuses. These days in cities, women might wear marriage symbols such as *sindoor* (vermillion), *choori* (bangles), *bindi* (red dot on forehead), and *mangal-sootra* (wedding necklace) as adornment (fashion), but they do not believe in those symbols anymore. There is no time or need to put a question mark on their beliefs. In this age of independence, everyone is free to live their own lives.

In our culture, many religious and social customs have scientific importance. The marriage symbols, carried on as tradition in different regions of the country, have special scientific significance too.

In an effort to be civilized, humans are becoming social by taking along the diversity and similarity in their personal lives. These diversities and similarities have their own identity. Different religions and castes can be identified by their symbolic marks. But those symbols never competed with each other. They never became a cause of social dissolution. People from different religions and castes kept wearing and decorating themselves with their own identification marks. They were proud to identify themselves with a certain religion or caste by wearing the associated symbols. One of those symbols was the last name associated with a caste. These symbols were recognized on an international level and they keep making their identities. They are an important device of the social system, and from time-to-time movements rose to abolish them. But it was not so easy to uproot the symbols that are rooted deep in the hearts of society. In this way, the symbols have continued to be abandoned at times, and at other times, there have been social efforts to urge people to continue wearing them.

On studying these social aspects, one finds that these symbols are not just for the identification of religion or caste, neither are they for adornment. The truth is that the things or daily rituals needed for a human being's good health are not adopted if they are conveyed only as health-related things. But the society adopts them when they are told about their importance in religious rituals or customs.

Praying to the sun, taking a bath in a holy river, planting *tulsi* (holy basil) in front of your house and watering it every day—these are all religious rituals. These activities, however, are more related to a person's health. In the same way, wearing the many marriage symbols, men and women have begun to forget the health benefits associated with them. They only remember the religious aspects of the symbols. It is as if a married woman forgets to put *sindoor* (vermillion) in her hair before eating the first meal of the day, then her mind is filled with a foreboding. If a married woman's wrists are without bangles even for a moment, she quickly hides them in the corner of her saree, fearing it to be a bad omen.

Recently I found myself in a problematic situation. While going through the security check at the Rashtrapati Bhavan (President's House), the young woman security guard brushed my feet in the process. She was just doing her job, but blessings came out of my mouth automatically, "*Saubhagyavati raho!*" (Stay married forever).

After blessing her, I became a little nervous. She neither had *sindoor* in her hair, nor a *mangal-sootra* (wedding necklace) around her neck. But she was delighted with my blessing. She said, "Thank you, Madam. Many madams get angry, but you blessed me."

I sighed with relief and asked, "Are you married?"

She replied immediately, "Of course. That is why you blessed me to stay married." It is not permissible to linger in that spot for long, so I walked ahead. But one thought kept brewing in my mind. Our society has such a nice system. On seeing a woman, you can immediately ascertain their marital status. You can identify them as unmarried, married, or a widow. And the emotions the viewers feel towards them are in accordance with their status. You can begin an appropriate conversation with a stranger based on their marital status.

These days, without much thought, there is a trend to abandon these symbols in the name of modernism. There is also an illusion being spread that our traditional customs and rituals bear no relation to science. That these are orthodox ways of life, a hoax, or symbols of women's enslavement.

But my guess is that many traditions of our family life are, in fact, scientific, and the marriage symbols must have been invented by health specialists. Just like nose and ear piercings and wearing rings or studs in them are now considered scientific. Wearing a *hasuli* (wide metallic necklace) on the neck, *bichhua* (toe rings) in the toes, *jhanjhar* (anklets) on the ankles—are said to have health benefits.

Let us think about some of the marriage symbols. The symbols are, in fact, different in different parts of the country. In the North and the East, the common symbols are *sindoor* (vermillion), glass bangles, and toe-rings, whereas in the South and the West, *mangal-sootra* (wedding necklace) and toe-rings are common, and in the state of Kashmir *athoor* (ornament worn on the ears) is a common symbol. There are religion-based identification marks too—Christians use wedding bands on a particular finger and married Muslim women wear glass bangles and blacken their teeth with *missi* (miswak is used for oral hygiene). In conversations and by observation it seems that even the Muslim women in Eastern

Uttar Pradesh and Bihar are wearing *sindoor* and glass bangles. In Maharashtra, Muslim women have started to wear *mangal-sootra*. Commonality is pervasive in the customs and rituals of social life. Even in Hindu families these days, the exchange of rings before the wedding has become custom.

Sindoor in the hair and *bindi* on the forehead, or something else—different places have different adornments as marriage symbols. These become the identification of a married woman. A woman adorning these is considered beautiful in the eyes of society. It is an adornment as well as a belief. And an identification mark too. A friend of mine became a widow at a young age. She did not stop wearing a red *bindi* (dot on the forehead). People used to find it strange. But she continued wearing the marriage symbols without caring about the society.

One day she said to me, "I keep wearing the marriage symbols so that people in stores and offices assume I am a married woman. The world is not kind to a young and beautiful widow."

Hearing this, I realized that these symbols are also an armor. It is a different matter that these days, in the name of fashion, even the married women do not wear these symbols. Perhaps they hope to continue being taken for single women. Or perhaps it is a first step towards breaking the relationship. Young women moving forward in their competitive frenzy against men have started saying, "Why should only we adorn these symbols? Why not the husbands? Why should only the women fast on Karva Chauth and Hartalika Teej (married women observe a fast on these days and pray for their husbands' long lives)? Why don't the husbands do it too?"

The women are competing to be equal with the men. They are uncomfortable. What should be said to them? One thing is certain that these symbols also strengthen one's belief in the marriage institution. Every time a married woman wears *sindoor* in her hair-parting, puts a red *bindi* on her forehead, or wears a *mangal-sootra* in her neck, she is reminded of her marital responsibilities.

It is believed that before the *sindoor* is applied, hair should be parted in the middle of the scalp. No hair should cross the parting from one side to another. In the Mithilanchal region, a *bhabhi* (brother's wife), sister, or *bua* (father's sister) helped to ensure that the bride's hair was parted in a straight line during the *sindoor* ceremony in a wedding. The woman who helps was gifted a *saree* from the groom's side, and it is known as the "*baat-fadai saree*" (saree for hair-parting).

There is a scientific belief that *sindoor* contains mercury or quicksilver. A straight parting through the center of the crown reaches *bramha-randhra* (a crevice in the crown of the head from which God is said to enter the human body). It is believed to awaken *kundalini*, a latent female energy. The color red (of the *sindoor*) is meant to make consciousness glow. That is why it is forbidden for unmarried girls.

According to color science, the red color awakens masculinity. Yellow is a symbol of renunciation. White signifies peace. Blue and black color ignite *tamas* energy, the energy of darkness, inactivity, and materiality. A woman's adornments involve a sense of *tamas* too. The kohl in a woman's eyes has *tamas*.

All these symbols not only adorn a woman, but they also invoke the belief system.

Across the states of Maharashtra, Andhra Pradesh, Tamil Nadu, Kerela, Karnataka, and Goa—the *mangal-sootra* is a common marriage symbol, although there are slight variations from one state to another. It is a symbol of the union of two families. Married women wear a necklace made of gold and black beads (*mangal-sootra*). But the most important part of the necklace is the pendant which has two small bowl-shaped pieces. One bowl represents the groom's side and the other the bride's side. In Maharashtra, they keep turmeric in one bowl and *sindoor* (*kumkum;* vermillion) in another. The pendant is strung in a red thread and the bride wears it around her neck. A month and a half after the wedding, the pendant bowls are turned upside down, and it is worn in a necklace of black and gold beads.

In Andhra, the two bowls are called *taari.* There is a red coral bead in the center joining the two bowls. This is how the *mangal-sootra* represents the union of two families. Another name for a woman is *duhita*—one who benefits two families. The *mangal-sootra* also has gold pieces with engraved images of the family Gods (*kul devta*) of the two families. This is how the woman, seeing the necklace hanging on her neck, touching her heart, is reminded of her role as a link between the two families. Married women in Bengal wear *pola* (red bangles) and bracelets made of elephant tusk. They also wear *sindoor* and glass bangles, and *bichhua* (toe rings) too. Married women in Rajasthan wear *borla* (jewelry worn in the hair-parting) on their forehead. It looks beautiful. Their bangles are special as well.

In Bihar and Uttar Pradesh, toe rings on the middle toe and bangles made of either glass or lac are required. In Bihar too, before the *sindoor* ceremony, the bride is made to wear a gold pendant (*dholna*) which comes from the groom's side. It can be taken off after a month and a half. *Dholna* is a small half-inch long gold cylinder, strung in a red thread. It is similar to a *mangal-sootra.* But the married women in Bihar are not required to wear it at all times.

In our culture, there is a special importance placed on the *grihastha ashram* (the family phase of life), which is based on a person's married life. The other three phases of life—*bramhacharya* (the student phase), *vaanprastha* (the retired life), and *sanyas* (life of renunciation) depend on this important phase. The marriage symbols have an important significance in leading a married life, and they should continue to be important. It is our responsibility to help our new generation adopt these beliefs. The Indian culture is rooted in these beliefs which make our culture everlasting.

I hope you get the message I am trying to convey with this long preamble.

Blessings,
Your Mom

□□□